On Happiness

ARISTOTLE

On Happiness

NICOMACHEAN ETHICS ◆ BOOK X

Translated by
H. Rackham

With an Introduction by
Piet Gerbrandy

AIORA

Cover artwork by Panagiotis Stavropoulos
Ink on recycled paper produced by Kyra Stratoudaki

© Aiora Press 2023

All rights reserved. No part of this publication may be reproduced, stored in a retrieval system, or transmitted, in any form or by any means, electronic, mechanical, photocopying, recording or otherwise, without written permission of the publishers.

First edition June 2023
Reprinted July 2024

ISBN: 978-618-5369-72-9

AIORA PRESS
11 Mavromichali st.
Athens 10679 - Greece
tel: +30 210 3839000
www.aiorabooks.com

Contents

Introduction 9

On Happiness
NICOMACHEAN ETHICS BOOK X 25

Further Reading 127

Introduction

THE PURSUIT OF HAPPINESS

One of the most compelling political statements of principle of all time is the American Declaration of Independence of 4 July 1776. In the so-called free West the second sentence of this declaration has been quoted so often that we now seldom stop to think about what it actually says. It reads as follows:

> We hold these truths to be self-evident, that all men are created equal, that they are endowed by their Creator with certain unalienable Rights, that among these are Life, Liberty and the pursuit of Happiness.

Are these truths really so self-evident? Apart from the question to what extent the rights listed

have been endowed by a divine being, we must conclude that in reality there is not so much equality and that the right to life and liberty is not universally acknowledged, let alone respected. And what did the Founding Fathers actually mean by happiness?

Political ideals are usually based on values regarded as absolute, which in turn are embedded in visions of the 'essence' of humanity. Although we may agree historically and globally on a few typical characteristics of human beings, for instance that in principle we are creatures that can think and that live in groups, it appears that any further definition is in fact highly culture-specific. Many branches of science and scholarship, from biology and anthropology to law and literature, examine who we believe we are and how we live, and how much diversity there is in this.

However, there is also a branch of knowledge—if we can call it that—which asks how we *should* live: this is ethics, traditionally one of the most important fields of philosophy and without doubt the philosophical discipline that is most focused on application in daily life. Because everyday life usually takes place in a community, ethics and politics are closely

connected. Clearly, the answer to the question of what a good life entails depends to a very large extent on the cultural and socio-economic circumstances in which the researcher is operating. Exploring what thinkers in various periods and language areas have said—often quite categorically—about human beings, happiness and society sharpens our understanding of the diversity of views and encourages us to be circumspect, since although we are constantly faced with crucial choices, we don't really know how we should live. And that happiness we are supposedly all pursuing—what might that actually be?

Few books are so suited to stimulating critical thought about the good life as Aristotle's *Nicomachean Ethics*, the tenth and final book of which is presented here. In order to understand what Aristotle says, it is important to provide some context. I will therefore briefly discuss the man, the world he lived in and the oeuvre attributed to him, and then provide an outline of the *Ethics* as a whole and more specifically of Book 10.

Aristotle, born in 384 BCE in northern Greece, studied at the Academy in Athens with Plato, eventually

becoming a leading fellow researcher. After the death of his teacher in 347 BCE Aristotle went travelling to conduct research. We know that he lived on Lesbos for a few years studying the anatomy of plants and animals there and thus inventing the science of biology. In 342 BCE he was invited to tutor the crown prince of Macedonia, then about fourteen years old, who was later to become Alexander the Great. Aristotle accepted the job, but it is not clear how long he stayed in Pella. Upon his return to Athens he founded his own school and research institute, the Lyceum (or the Peripatos). In 323 BCE he left Athens and he died a year later on the island of Euboea.

Aristotle must have published many works during his lifetime, but they have all been lost; we only know a few titles. The large corpus attributed to him that has been passed down was not intended for publication. It consists of treatises or essays of varying length and detail, possibly notes for his lectures, which were probably compiled into complete works partly by Aristotle himself and partly by later associates at the Lyceum. That Aristotle saw his oeuvre as a coherent whole is shown by the fact

that he frequently refers to his own writings. In the centuries after Aristotle's death the corpus was lost for some time and only resurfaced again in the middle of the first century BCE, in Rome, where the politician and philosopher Cicero had access to it. From that point onwards Aristotle was studied rigorously and extensive commentaries were delivered on his work until the early Middle Ages. After the triumph of the Arabs it was translated into Arabic, sometimes via Syriac. It was only in the course of the twelfth century that Aristotle's oeuvre again became available in the West, translated directly from Greek into Latin, often along with Arabic commentaries, also translated. Thinkers such as Thomas Aquinas (1225–1274) integrated Aristotelian ideas into Christian theology, thus creating a school of philosophy known as scholasticism, which was to dominate thinking within the Catholic Church for centuries.

It is hard to think of a branch of science or philosophy to which Aristotle did *not* contribute; in fact, he may be regarded as the founder of Western science. He wrote works in the fields of metaphysics and physics, logic and the philosophy of language,

biology and psychology, poetry and rhetoric, political science and ethics. A characteristic feature of his method is that he always thoroughly examined what had already been written or said about the subject in question (including of course by Plato, who is sometimes severely criticized though without mention of his name), that he worked by analysing and classifying, and that he usually tested his theories against reality. A compelling example of his empirical approach is that he had his students document the constitutions of no fewer than 158 different city states (unfortunately only that of Athens has survived). This project served as the basis of his political theory.

Aristotle expressly regarded ethics as a domain closely linked to politics. According to him, man is a *zôion politikon*, as he says in his *Politics*: a social creature, or rather, a creature that belongs to a community. But what is a community, or a *polis*, to use the Greek term usually translated as 'city', 'state' or 'city-state'? As a northerner in Athens, to a certain extent Aristotle was an outsider, which enabled him to think critically about the nature of life as a citizen. However, this relative distance did not

exclude certain blind spots. Even nominally democratic Athens was a class society with considerable inequality as regards wealth, power and knowledge. Women were excluded from active citizenship, the heavy work was done by slaves (often non-Greeks) and immigrants had very limited rights. Aristotle, who was not an Athenian but did belong to an affluent class of intellectuals, seems to have regarded social inequality as a given. As we shall see, this had an impact on his view of the good life.

Two works by Aristotle on ethics have survived: the *Nicomachean Ethics* and the *Eudemian Ethics*. There is considerable overlap between the works, which may suggest that even in antiquity editors had varying opinions as to the best way to organize the material about ethics. However, generally the *Nicomachean Ethics* is regarded as the most mature and complete treatise. At some points the structure of the work as a whole is not entirely clear; it is striking, for instance, that Aristotle discusses the phenomenon of *hêdonê* (pleasure) in two separate passages without those passages referring to each other. Might one of these be a separate essay that

was later inserted into the larger work by Aristotle himself or an editor? However, it is not really a problem, because anyone who reads the work from cover to cover will certainly experience it as being a coherent whole. This does not mean it is an easy work; often Aristotle seems to be thinking out loud (you can see him developing thoughts before your eyes), and as a result he occasionally takes a side path that is not marked as such. If a modern author were to submit a manuscript like this to their publisher, it would be thoroughly edited.

It is worth mentioning that the division into books (scrolls) dates from antiquity and in most cases was clearly intended by Aristotle himself, but that the division into chapters dates from much later. In any event, the *Ethics* (as I will refer to the work from this point on) is a whole, with a beginning and an end, since the conclusion wraps up a discussion that began in the first chapters of Book 1.

The *Ethics* opens with the proposition that every form of activity is aimed at some end (*telos*), which is regarded as something good. Many ends may in turn serve as means to a higher end, which raises the question whether there might be an ultimate

end, something towards which all human activity ultimately strives. Aristotle asserts that we agree that this supreme good is *eudaimonia*, a word usually translated as 'happiness'. In Aristotle's view, it is a state of being that is sufficient in itself and is not a means to attain something else. Etymologically, *eudaimonia* refers to a situation in which the gods (*daimones*) ensure that you fare well (*eu*). At least since the Romantic era we have been accustomed to associate happiness with pleasant feelings, but *eudaimonia* has little or nothing to do with emotions. *Eudaimonia* is a successful life, a life in which for a long period, preferably as long as you are on this earth, you manage to achieve that which you value most. Aristotle sees *eudaimonia* not as a stable condition of well-being, but as an activity (*energeia*) aimed at reaching one's full potential (*dynamis*).

In practice people differ as regards what they value the most. Aristotle distinguishes three categories. Firstly there is the group that equates happiness as a life in the service of *hêdonê*. This concept covers the entire spectrum of pleasant experiences, from joy and satisfaction, to delight and pleasure. A person experiencing *hêdonê* feels good. Aristotle

deeply despises people who regard this as their highest goal, since creatures without reason, such as children and animals, also strive towards pleasure. The second category consists of those devoted to political ambitions: they want to gain power and honour, while often claiming that they are using their excellence (*aretê*) to improve society. Aristotle certainly approves of this group, because he is aware that people in fact belong to a *polis*, so that it is best to make sure you behave as honourably as possible within that community. But true happiness is only to be found among the third category: the men (as it did not occur to Aristotle that women might also be able to make this choice) who devote their life to philosophical contemplation (*theôria*). Man is after all a rational being; what distinguishes him from animals is *nous*, the ability to think clearly. A person who wants to fulfil their potential as a human being perfectly will arrange their life in such a way that they can devote all their time and attention to thought.

Notably, most of the *Ethics* is not about this last group, which of course Aristotle realizes is extremely small. A topic the book does examine at length is

the requirements for a successful life within the *polis*. For this one needs not so much philosophical wisdom as practical wisdom or prudence (*phronêsis*), a form of clear thinking aimed at organizing your own life and that of your family and fellow citizens as wisely as possible. *Phronêsis* is not separated from virtue or moral excellence (*aretê*), which is not so much an attribute as an inner state or disposition (*hexis*) developed through upbringing and training. Both parents and state institutions have a duty to raise young people to be citizens who are sensible and of high moral calibre.

More than four books are devoted to discussing the main civic virtues (bravery, moderation, generosity, justice). Aristotle observes that they can often be regarded as a mean between two extremes: bravery is between cowardice and recklessness, generosity between avarice and a tendency towards extravagance. Books 8 and 9 are about friendship, an indispensable component of a successful life within the *polis*.

But then comes Book 10, which consists of two halves (apart from the last chapter, which forms the transition to Aristotle's *Politics*). The first five

chapters discuss *hêdonê,* something the reader, given the beginning of Book 1, would probably not have expected. The next four chapters return to the thinking life of the philosopher.

Unlike in Book 1, here Aristotle does not reject *hêdonê*. After analysing the views of other thinkers, he concludes that it can be a by-product of other activities. Acting well for the benefit of the community is also pleasurable, and the same is even more true of philosophical contemplation. *Hêdonê* completes those actions and may therefore provide an incentive to continue to perform them. But Aristotle stresses that this form of pleasure must not be confused with physical pleasure or amusement: man is born for worthier activities.

The highest form of *eudaimonia* is that of the philosopher. While a philosopher must eat and drink, and have some clothes and a roof over his head, he does not really need anything else. Assuming that in the cosmic order man occupies a place halfway between animals and gods, it is essential to develop that which is most divine in us to the fullest, and that is thinking. After all, that is the activity that characterizes the gods: their happiness

consists of uninterrupted philosophical contemplation. Anyone who derives *hêdonê* from this will have to admit that this particular pleasure is a good thing.

As Aristotle describes it, this contemplative state of being sounds extraordinarily appealing, but the scientist in him is realistic enough to understand that only a small elite of wealthy people can afford such a life. After all, we are not gods; we have to eat, fund the maintenance of our house, eliminate our enemies and raise our children, and, whether we like or not, we need friendship, if only to share philosophical insights and to become wiser from doing so. Even the philosopher is a citizen, and in view of that fact it makes sense for him to use his intellectual and moral attributes for the benefit of the community. Perhaps this kind of life comes second, but it too can be called a successful life.

What makes the *Ethics* so instructive and appealing is that in spite of his high ideals, Aristotle always remains realistic and doesn't absolutize anything, because given his empirical approach he is constantly looking around him and testing his ideas

against commonly and less commonly held views. However, the most important insight to be gained from reading this work is the idea that happiness is not a comfortable state of well-being, but an energetic and carefully considered endeavour to lead a rich and meaningful life. Probably that is also what the authors of the *Declaration of Independence* had in mind.

Piet Gerbrandy

Translated from the Dutch
by Margaret Kofod

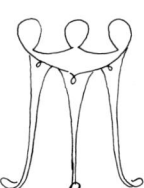

Ἠθικὰ Νικομάχεια

ΒΙΒΛΙΟΝ Κ

Nicomachean Ethics
BOOK X

I Μετὰ δὲ ταῦτα περὶ ἡδονῆς ἴσως ἕπεται διελθεῖν. μάλιστα γὰρ δοκεῖ συνῳκειῶσθαι τῷ γένει ἡμῶν· διὸ παιδεύουσι τοὺς νέους οἰακίζοντες ἡδονῇ καὶ λύπῃ. δοκεῖ δὲ καὶ πρὸς τὴν τοῦ ἤθους ἀρετὴν μέγιστον εἶναι τὸ χαίρειν οἷς δεῖ καὶ μισεῖν ἃ δεῖ· διατείνει γὰρ ταῦτα διὰ παντὸς τοῦ βίου, ῥοπὴν ἔχοντα καὶ δύναμιν πρὸς ἀρετήν τε καὶ τὸν εὐδαίμονα βίον· τὰ μὲν γὰρ ἡδέα προαιροῦνται, τὰ δὲ λυπηρὰ φεύγουσιν. ὑπὲρ δὴ τῶν τοιούτων ἥκιστ' ἂν δόξειε παρετέον εἶναι, ἄλλως τε καὶ πολλὴν ἐχόντων ἀμφισβήτησιν. οἱ μὲν γὰρ τἀγαθὸν ἡδονὴν λέγουσιν, οἱ δ' ἐξ ἐνα-

Our next business after this is doubtless to discuss Pleasure. For pleasure is thought to be especially congenial to mankind; and this is why pleasure and pain are employed in the education of the young, as means whereby to steer their course. Moreover, to like and to dislike the right things is thought to be a most important element in the formation of a virtuous character. For pleasure and pain extend throughout the whole of life, and are of great moment and influence for virtue and happiness; since men choose what is pleasant and avoid what is painful.

It would therefore seem by no means proper to omit so important a subject, especially as there is much difference of opinion about it. Some people maintain that pleasure is the Good. Others on the

ντίας κομιδῇ φαῦλον, οἱ μὲν ἴσως πεπεισμένοι οὕτω καὶ ἔχειν, οἱ δὲ οἰόμενοι βέλτιον εἶναι πρὸς τὸν βίον ἡμῶν ἀποφαίνειν τὴν ἡδονὴν τῶν φαύλων, καὶ εἰ μὴ ἐστίν· ῥέπειν γὰρ τοὺς πολλοὺς πρὸς αὐτὴν καὶ δουλεύειν ταῖς ἡδοναῖς, διὸ δεῖν εἰς τοὐναντίον ἄγειν· ἐλθεῖν γὰρ ἂν οὕτως ἐπὶ τὸ μέσον. μή ποτε δὲ οὐ καλῶς τοῦτο λέγεται. οἱ γὰρ περὶ τῶν ἐν τοῖς πάθεσι καὶ ταῖς πράξεσι λόγοι ἧττόν εἰσι πιστοὶ τῶν ἔργων· ὅταν οὖν διαφωνῶσι τοῖς κατὰ τὴν αἴσθησιν, καταφρονούμενοι καὶ τἀληθὲς προσαναιροῦσιν· ὁ γὰρ ψέγων τὴν ἡδονήν, ὀφθείς ποτ' ἐφιέμενος, ἀποκλίνειν δοκεῖ πρὸς αὐτὴν ὡς τοιαύτην οὖσαν ἅπασαν· τὸ διορίζειν γὰρ οὐκ ἔστι τῶν πολλῶν. ἐοίκασιν οὖν οἱ ἀληθεῖς τῶν λόγων οὐ μόνον πρὸς τὸ εἰδέναι χρησιμώτατοι εἶναι, ἀλλὰ καὶ πρὸς τὸν βίον· συνῳδοὶ γὰρ ὄντες τοῖς ἔργοις πιστεύονται, διὸ

contrary say that it is altogether bad: some of them perhaps from a conviction that it is really so, but others because they think it to be in the interests of morality to make out that pleasure is bad, even if it is not, since most men (they argue) have a bias towards it, and are the slaves of their pleasures, so that they have to be driven in the opposite direction in order to arrive at the due mean.

Possibly however this view is mistaken. In matters of emotion and of action, words are less convincing than deeds; when therefore our theories are at variance with palpable facts, they provoke contempt, and involve the truth in their own discredit. If one who censures pleasure is seen sometimes to desire it himself, his swerving towards it is thought to show that he really believes that all pleasure is desirable; for the mass of mankind cannot discriminate. Hence it appears that true theories are the most valuable for conduct as well as for science; harmonizing with the facts, they carry conviction, and so encourage those who understand them to guide their lives by them.

προτρέπονται τοὺς ξυνιέντας ζῆν κατ᾽ αὐτούς. τῶν μὲν οὖν τοιούτων ἅλις, τὰ δ᾽ εἰρημένα περὶ τῆς ἡδονῆς ἐπέλθωμεν.

II Εὔδοξος μὲν οὖν τὴν ἡδονὴν τἀγαθὸν ᾤετ᾽ εἶναι διὰ τὸ πάνθ᾽ ὁρᾶν ἐφιέμενα αὐτῆς, καὶ ἔλλογα καὶ ἄλογα· ἐν πᾶσι δ᾽ εἶναι τὸ αἱρετὸν ἐπιεικές, καὶ τὸ μάλιστα κράτιστον· τὸ δὴ πάντ᾽ ἐπὶ ταὐτὸ φέρεσθαι μηνύειν ὡς πᾶσι τοῦτο ἄριστον (ἕκαστον γὰρ τὸ αὑτῷ ἀγαθὸν εὑρίσκειν, ὥσπερ καὶ τροφήν), τὸ δὲ πᾶσιν ἀγαθόν, καὶ οὗ πάντ᾽ ἐφίεται, τἀγαθὸν εἶναι. ἐπιστεύοντο δ᾽ οἱ λόγοι διὰ τὴν τοῦ ἤθους ἀρετὴν μᾶλλον ἢ δι᾽ αὑτούς· διαφερόντως γὰρ ἐδόκει σώφρων εἶναι· οὐ δὴ ὡς φίλος τῆς ἡδονῆς ἐδόκει ταῦτα λέγειν, ἀλλ᾽ οὕτως ἔχειν κατ᾽ ἀλήθειαν, — οὐχ ἧττον δ᾽ ᾤετ᾽ εἶναι φανερὸν ἐκ τοῦ ἐναντίου· τὴν γὰρ λύπην καθ᾽ αὑτὸ πᾶσι φευκτὸν εἶναι, ὁμοίως δὴ τοὐναντίον

With so much by way of introduction, let us now review the theories about pleasure that have been advanced.

That pleasure is the Good was held by Eudoxus, on the following grounds. He saw that all creatures, rational and irrational alike, seek to obtain it; but in every case (he argued) that which is desirable is good, and that which is most desirable is the best; therefore the fact that all creatures 'move in the direction of' the same thing indicates that this thing is the Supreme Good for all (since everything finds its own particular good, just as it finds its own proper food); but that which is good for all, and which all seek to obtain, is the Good.

His arguments owed their acceptance however more to the excellence of his character than to their own merit. He had the reputation of being a man of exceptional temperance, and hence he was not suspected of upholding this view because he was a lover of pleasure, but people thought it must really be true.

He also held that the goodness of pleasure was equally manifest from the converse: pain is intrinsi-

αἱρετόν, — μάλιστα δ' εἶναι αἱρετὸν ὃ μὴ δι' ἕτερον μηδ' ἑτέρου χάριν αἱρούμεθα· τοιοῦτον δ' ὁμολογουμένως εἶναι τὴν ἡδονήν· οὐδένα γὰρ ἐπερωτᾶν τίνος ἕνεκα ἥδεται, ὡς καθ' αὑτὴν οὖσαν αἱρετὴν τὴν ἡδονήν, — προστιθεμένην τε ὁτῳοῦν τῶν ἀγαθῶν αἱρετώτερον ποιεῖν, οἷον τῷ δικαιοπραγεῖν καὶ σωφρονεῖν· αὔξεσθαι δὲ τὸ ἀγαθὸν αὐτὸ αὑτῷ. ἔοικε δὴ οὗτός γε ὁ λόγος τῶν ἀγαθῶν αὐτὴν ἀποφαίνειν, καὶ οὐδὲν μᾶλλον ἑτέρου· πᾶν γὰρ μεθ' ἑτέρου ἀγαθοῦ αἱρετώτερον ἢ μονούμενον. τοιούτῳ δὴ λόγῳ καὶ Πλάτων ἀναιρεῖ ὅτι οὐκ ἔστιν ἡδονὴ τἀγαθόν· αἱρετώτερον γὰρ εἶναι τὸν ἡδὺν βίον μετὰ φρονήσεως ἢ χωρίς, εἰ δὲ τὸ μικτὸν κρεῖττον, οὐκ εἶναι τὴν ἡδονὴν τἀγαθόν· οὐδενὸς γὰρ προστεθέντος αὐτῷ τἀγαθὸν αἱρετώτερον γίνεσθαι. δῆλον δ' ὡς οὐδ' ἄλλο οὐδὲν τἀγαθὸν ἂν

cally an object of avoidance to all, therefore its opposite must be intrinsically an object of desire to all.

Again, he argued that that thing is most desirable which we choose not as a means to or for the sake of something else; but such admittedly is pleasure: we never ask a man for what purpose he indulges in pleasure—we assume it to be desirable in itself.

He also said that the addition of pleasure to any good—for instance, just or temperate conduct—makes that good more desirable; but only the good can enhance the good.

Now as for the last argument, it seems only to prove that pleasure is a good, and not that it is in any way better than any other good; for every good is more desirable when combined with some other good than in isolation. In fact, a similar argument is employed by Plato to refute the view that pleasure is the Good: the life of pleasure, he urges, is more desirable in combination with intelligence than without it; but if pleasure combined with something else is better than pleasure alone, it is not the Good, for the Good is not rendered more desirable by the addition of anything to it. And it is clear that nothing

εἴη, ὃ μετά τινος τῶν καθ' αὑτὰ ἀγαθῶν αἱρετώτερον γίνεται. τί οὖν ἐστὶ τοιοῦτον, οὗ καὶ ἡμεῖς κοινωνοῦμεν; τοιοῦτον γὰρ ἐπιζητεῖται.

Οἱ δ' ἐνιστάμενοι ὡς οὐκ ἀγαθὸν οὗ πάντ' ἐφίεται, μὴ οὐθὲν λέγουσιν· ἃ γὰρ πᾶσι δοκεῖ, ταῦτ' εἶναί φαμεν· ὁ δ' ἀναιρῶν ταύτην τὴν πίστιν οὐ πάνυ πιστότερα ἐρεῖ. εἰ μὲν γὰρ τὰ ἀνόητα μόνα ὠρέγετο αὐτῶν, ἦν ἄν τι τὸ λεγόμενον, εἰ δὲ καὶ τὰ φρόνιμα, πῶς λέγοιεν ἄν τι; ἴσως δὲ καὶ ἐν τοῖς φαύλοις ἐστί τι φυσικὸν [ἀγαθὸν] κρεῖττον ἢ καθ' αὑτά, ὃ ἐφίεται τοῦ οἰκείου ἀγαθοῦ. — οὐκ ἔοικε δὲ οὐδὲ περὶ τοῦ ἐναντίου καλῶς λέγεσθαι. οὐ γάρ φασιν, εἰ ἡ λύπη κακόν ἐστι, τὴν ἡδονὴν ἀγαθὸν εἶναι· ἀντικεῖσθαι γὰρ καὶ κακὸν κακῷ καὶ [ἄμφω] τῷ μηδετέρῳ — λέγοντες ταῦτα οὐ κακῶς, οὐ μὴν ἐπί γε τῶν εἰρημένων ἀλη-

else either will be the Good if it becomes more desirable when combined with something good in itself. What thing is there then of this nature, which is attainable by us? for it is something of this nature that we are in search of.

Those on the other hand who deny that that which all creatures seek to obtain is good, are surely talking nonsense. For what all think to be good, that, we assert, is good; and he that subverts our belief in the opinion of all mankind, will hardly persuade us to believe his own either. If only the irrational creatures strove to obtain what is pleasant, there would have been some sense in this contention; but inasmuch as beings endowed with intelligence do so too, how can it be right? And perhaps even the lower animals possess an instinct superior to their own natures, which seeks to obtain the good appropriate to their kind.

Again, these thinkers' refutation of the argument from the converse appears equally unsound. They pain say, if pain is bad, it does not follow therefore that pleasure is good: for an evil can also be opposed to an evil and to a thing that is neither

θεύοντες. ἀμφοῖν μὲν γὰρ ὄντοιν <τῶν> κακῶν καὶ φευκτὰ ἔδει ἄμφω εἶναι, τῶν μηδετέρων δὲ μηδέτερον ἢ ὁμοίως· νῦν δὲ φαίνονται τὴν μὲν φεύγοντες ὡς κακόν, τὴν δ' αἱρούμενοι ὡς ἀγαθόν· οὕτω δὴ καὶ ἀντίκειται.

III Οὐ μὴν οὐδ' εἰ μὴ τῶν ποιοτήτων ἐστὶν ἡ ἡδονή, διὰ τοῦτ' οὐδὲ τῶν ἀγαθῶν· οὐδὲ γὰρ αἱ τῆς ἀρετῆς ἐνέργειαι ποιότητές εἰσιν, οὐδ' ἡ εὐδαιμονία. — λέγουσι δὲ τὸ μὲν ἀγαθὸν ὡρίσθαι, τὴν δ' ἡδονὴν ἀόριστον εἶναι, ὅτι δέχεται τὸ μᾶλλον καὶ [τὸ] ἧττον. εἰ μὲν οὖν ἐκ τοῦ ἥδεσθαι τοῦτο κρίνουσι, καὶ περὶ τὴν δικαιοσύνην καὶ τὰς ἄλλας ἀρετάς, καθ' ἃς ἐναργῶς φασὶ μᾶλλον καὶ ἧττον [τοὺς] ποιοὺς [ὑπάρχειν καὶ κατὰ τὰς ἀρετάς], ἔσται τὸ αὐτό (δίκαιοι γάρ εἰσι μᾶλλον καὶ ἀνδρεῖοι,

good nor evil: a statement which is indeed sound enough, but which does not apply to the things in question. If both pleasure and pain were in the class of evils, both would be also of necessity things to be avoided, and if in the class of things neutral, neither ought to be avoided, or they ought to be avoided alike; but as it is we see men avoid pain as evil and choose pleasure as good; it is therefore as good and evil that they are opposed.

Nor yet does it follow that if pleasure is not a quality, therefore it is not a good. Virtuous activities are not qualities either, nor is happiness.

Again they argue that good is definite, but that pleasure is indefinite, because it admits of degrees. Now (a) if they base this judgement on the fact that one can be more or less pleased, the same argument will apply to Justice and the other virtues, the possessors of which are clearly spoken of as being more or less virtuous; for example, A may be more just or brave, and may act more, or less, justly or temperately, than B. If on the other hand (b) they judge by the nature of the pleasures themselves, I am afraid they do not state the right ground for

ἔστι δὲ καὶ δικαιοπραγεῖν καὶ σωφρονεῖν μᾶλλον καὶ ἧττον)· εἰ δὲ ταῖς ἡδοναῖς, μή ποτ' οὐ λέγουσι τὸ αἴτιον, ἂν ὦσιν αἱ μὲν ἀμιγεῖς αἱ δὲ μικταί. τί δε κωλύει, καθάπερ ὑγίεια ὡρισμένη οὖσα δέχεται τὸ μᾶλλον καὶ [τὸ] ἧττον, οὕτω καὶ τὴν ἡδονήν; οὐ γὰρ ἡ αὐτὴ συμμετρία ἐν πᾶσίν ἐστιν· οὐδ' ἐν τῷ αὐτῷ μία τις ἀεί, ἀλλ' ἀνιεμένη διαμένει ἕως τινός, καὶ διαφέρει τῷ μᾶλλον καὶ ἧττον. τοιοῦτον δὴ καὶ τὸ περὶ τὴν ἡδονὴν ἐνδέχεται εἶναι. — τέλειόν τε τἀγαθὸν τιθέντες, τὰς δὲ κινήσεις καὶ τὰς γενέσεις ἀτελεῖς, τὴν ἡδονὴν κίνησιν καὶ γένεσιν ἀποφαίνειν πειρῶνται. οὐ καλῶς δ' ἐοίκασι λέγειν, οὐδ' εἶναι κίνησις· πάσῃ γὰρ οἰκεῖον εἶναι δοκεῖ τάχος καὶ βραδυτής, καὶ εἰ μὴ καθ' αὑτήν, οἷον τῇ τοῦ κόσμου, πρὸς ἄλλο· τῇ δ' ἡδονῇ τούτων οὐδέτερον ὑπάρχει· ἡσθῆναι μὲν γὰρ ἔστι ταχέως ὥσπερ

their conclusion, if it be true that there are two kinds of pleasures, unmixed as well as mixed.

Again, (c) why should not pleasure be like health, which is definite although it admits of degrees? For health is not constituted by the same proportion of elements in all persons; nor yet by one particular proportion in the same person always, but when it is in process of dissolution it still lasts for a certain time, and therefore it varies in degree. It is possible therefore that the same may be the case with pleasure.

Again, they postulate that the Good is perfect, whereas a motion or process of generation is imperfect, and then they attempt to prove that pleasure is a motion or process. This appears to be a mistake. (a) It would seem that pleasure is not a motion; for we hold it to be a property of all motion to be quick or slow—if (as with the motion of the firmament) not absolutely, then relatively to some other moving body. But pleasure possesses neither absolute nor relative velocity. You can become pleased quickly, just as you can get angry quickly: but you cannot be pleased quickly, nor yet more

ὀργισθῆναι, ἥδεσθαι δ' οὔ, οὐδὲ πρὸς ἕτερον, βαδίζειν δὲ καὶ αὔξεσθαι καὶ πάντα τὰ τοιαῦτα. μεταβάλλειν μὲν οὖν εἰς τὴν ἡδονὴν ταχέως καὶ βραδέως ἔστιν, ἐνεργεῖν δὲ κατ' αὐτὴν οὐκ ἔστι ταχέως, λέγω δ' ἥδεσθαι. γένεσίς τε πῶς ἂν εἴη; δοκεῖ γὰρ οὐκ ἐκ τοῦ τυχόντος τὸ τυχὸν γίγνεσθαι, ἀλλ' ἐξ οὗ γίνεται, εἰς τοῦτο διαλύεσθαι· καὶ οὗ γένεσις ἡ ἡδονή, τούτου ἡ λύπη φθορά. — καὶ λέγουσι δὲ τὴν μὲν λύπην ἔνδειαν τοῦ κατὰ φύσιν εἶναι, τὴν δ' ἡδονὴν ἀναπλήρωσιν. ταῦτα δὲ σωματικά ἐστι τὰ πάθη. εἰ δή ἐστι τοῦ κατὰ φύσιν ἀναπλήρωσις ἡ ἡδονή, ἐν ᾧ ἡ ἀναπλήρωσις, τοῦτ' ἂν καὶ ἥδοιτο· τὸ σῶμα ἄρα· οὐ δοκεῖ δέ· οὐκ' ἔστιν ἄρα ἀναπλήρωσις ἡ ἡδονή, ἀλλὰ γινομένης μὲν ἀναπληρώσεως ἥδοιτ' ἄν τις, καὶ τεμνόμενος λυποῖτο. ἡ δόξα δ' αὕτη δοκεῖ γεγενῆσθαι ἐκ τῶν περὶ τὴν τροφὴν λυπῶν καὶ ἡδο-

quickly than somebody else, as you can walk, grow, etc., more quickly than somebody else. It is possible to pass into a pleasurable state quickly or slowly, but not to function in that state—i.e. to feel pleasure—quickly. And (b) in what sense can pleasure be a process of generation? We do not think that any chance thing can be generated from any other chance thing, but that a thing at its dissolution is resolved into that from which it is generated; and if pleasure is the generation of something, pain is the destruction of that thing. Also (c) they say that pain is a deficiency of the natural state and pleasure is its replenishment. But these are bodily experiences. Now if pleasure is a replenishment of the natural state, the pleasure will be felt by the thing in which the replenishment takes place. Therefore it is the body that feels pleasure. But this does not seem to be the case. Therefore pleasure is not a process of replenishment, though while replenishment takes place, a feeling of pleasure may accompany it, just as a feeling of pain may accompany a surgical operation. The belief that pleasure is a replenishment seems to have arisen from the pains and pleasures

νῶν· ἐνδεεῖς γὰρ γενομένους καὶ προλυπηθέντας ἥδεσθαι τῇ ἀναπληρώσει. τοῦτο δ' οὐ περὶ πάσας συμβαίνει τὰς ἡδονάς· ἄλυποι γάρ εἰσιν αἵ τε μαθηματικαὶ καὶ τῶν κατὰ τὰς αἰσθήσεις αἱ διὰ τῆς ὀσφρήσεως, καὶ ἀκροάματα δὲ καὶ ὁράματα πολλά, καὶ μνῆμαι καὶ ἐλπίδες. τίνος οὖν αὗται γενέσεις ἔσονται; οὐδενὸς γὰρ ἔνδεια γεγένηται, οὗ γένοιτ' ἂν ἀναπλήρωσις. —πρὸς δὲ τοὺς προφέροντας τὰς ἐπονειδίστους τῶν ἡδονῶν λέγοι τις ἂν ὅτι οὐκ ἔστι ταῦθ' ἡδέα· οὐ γὰρ εἰ τοῖς κακῶς διακειμένοις ἡδέα ἐστίν, οἰητέον αὐτὰ καὶ ἡδέα εἶναι πλὴν τούτοις, καθάπερ οὐδὲ τὰ τοῖς κάμνουσιν ὑγιεινὰ ἢ γλυκέα ἢ πικρά, οὐδ' αὖ λευκὰ τὰ φαινόμενα τοῖς ὀφθαλμιῶσιν. ἢ οὕτω λέγοι τις ἄν, ὅτι αἱ μὲν ἡδοναὶ αἱρεταί εἰσιν, οὐ μὴν ἀπό γε τούτων, ὥσπερ καὶ τὸ πλουτεῖν, προδόντι δ' οὔ, καὶ τὸ ὑγιαίνειν,

connected with food: here the pleasure does arise from a replenishment, and is preceded by the pain of a want. But this is not the case with all pleasures: the pleasures of knowledge, for example, have no antecedent pain; nor have certain of the pleasures of sense, namely those whose medium is the sense of smell, as well as many sounds and sights; and also memories and hopes. If these are processes of generation, generation of what? No lack of anything has occurred that may be replenished.

In reply to those who bring forward the disreputable pleasures, one may (a) deny that these are really pleasant: for granted they are pleasant to ill-conditioned people, it cannot therefore be assumed that they are actually pleasant, except to them, any more than things healthy or sweet or bitter to invalids are really so, or any more than things that seem white to people with a disease of the eyes are really white. Or (b) one may take the line that, though the pleasures themselves are desirable, they are not desirable when derived from those sources; just as wealth is desirable, but not if won by treachery, or health, but not at the cost of eating anything

οὐ μὴν ὁτιοῦν φαγόντι. ἢ τῷ εἴδει διαφέρουσιν αἱ ἡδοναί· ἕτεραι γὰρ αἱ ἀπὸ τῶν καλῶν τῶν ἀπὸ τῶν αἰσχρῶν, καὶ οὐκ ἔστιν ἡσθῆναι τὴν τοῦ δικαίου μὴ ὄντα δίκαιον οὐδὲ τὴν τοῦ μουσικοῦ μὴ ὄντα μουσικόν, ὁμοίως δὲ καὶ ἐπὶ τῶν ἄλλων. ἐμφανίζειν δὲ δοκεῖ καὶ ὁ φίλος, ἕτερος ὢν τοῦ κόλακος, οὐκ οὖσαν ἀγαθὸν τὴν ἡδονὴν ἢ διαφόρους εἴδει· ὁ μὲν γὰρ πρὸς τἀγαθὸν ὁμιλεῖν δοκεῖ, ὁ δὲ πρὸς ἡδονήν, καὶ τῷ μὲν ὀνειδίζεται, τὸν δ' ἐπαινοῦσιν ὡς πρὸς ἕτερα ὁμιλοῦντα. οὐδείς τ' ἂν ἕλοιτο ζῆν παιδίου διάνοιαν ἔχων διὰ βίου, ἡδόμενος ἐφ' οἷς τὰ παιδία ὡς οἷόν τε μάλιστα· οὐδὲ χαίρειν ποιῶν τι τῶν αἰσχίστων, μηδέποτε μέλλων λυπηθῆναι. περὶ πολλά τε σπουδὴν ποιησαίμεθ' ἂν καὶ εἰ μηδεμίαν ἐπιφέροι ἡδονήν, οἷον ὁρᾶν, μνημονεύειν, εἰδέναι, τὰς ἀρετὰς ἔχειν. εἰ δ' ἐξ ἀνάγκης ἕπονται

and everything. Or (c) we may say that pleasures differ in specific quality; since (α) those derived from noble sources are not the same as those derived from base sources, and it is impossible to feel the pleasures of a just man without being just, or the pleasures of a musician without being musical, and so on. And also (β) the distinction between a friend and a flatterer seems to show that pleasure is not a good, or else that pleasures are specifically different; since a friend is thought to aim at doing good to his companion, a flatterer at giving pleasure; to be a flatterer is a reproach, whereas a friend is praised because in his intercourse he aims at other things. And (γ) no one would choose to retain the mind of a child throughout his life, even though he continued to enjoy the pleasures of childhood with undiminished zest; nor (δ) would anyone choose to find enjoyment in doing some extremely shameful act, although it would entail no painful consequences. Also (ε) there are many things which we should be eager to possess even if they brought us no pleasure, for instance sight, memory, knowledge, virtue. It may be the case that

τούτοις ἡδοναί, οὐδὲν διαφέρει· ἑλοίμεθα γὰρ ἂν ταῦτα καὶ εἰ μὴ γίνοιτ' ἀπ' αὐτῶν ἡδονή. —ὅτι μὲν οὖν οὔτε τἀγαθὸν ἡ ἡδονὴ οὔτε πᾶσα αἱρετή, δῆλον ἔοικεν εἶναι, καὶ ὅτι εἰσί τινες αἱρεταὶ καθ' αὑτάς, διαφέρουσαι τῷ εἴδει ἢ ἀφ' ὧν. τὰ μὲν οὖν λεγόμενα περὶ τῆς ἡδονῆς καὶ λύπης ἱκανῶς εἰρήσθω.

IV Τί δ' ἐστὶν ἢ ποῖόν τι, καταφανέστερον γένοιτ' ἂν ἀπ' ἀρχῆς ἀναλαβοῦσιν. δοκεῖ γὰρ ἡ μὲν ὅρασις καθ' ὁντινοῦν χρόνον τελεία εἶναι· οὐ γάρ ἐστιν ἐνδεὴς οὐδενός, ὃ εἰς ὕστερον γενόμενον τελειώσει αὐτῆς τὸ εἶδος. τοιούτῳ δ' ἔοικε καὶ ἡ ἡδονή· ὅλον γάρ τί ἐστι, καὶ κατ' οὐδένα χρόνον λάβοι τις ἂν ἡδονὴν ἧς ἐπὶ πλείω χρόνον γινομένης τελειωθήσεται τὸ εἶδος. διόπερ οὐδὲ κίνησίς ἐστιν· ἐν χρόνῳ γὰρ πᾶσα κίνησις καὶ τέλους τινός, οἷον ἡ

these things are necessarily attended by pleasure, but that makes no difference; for we should desire them even if no pleasure resulted from them.

It seems therefore that pleasure is not the Good, and that not every pleasure is desirable, but also that there are certain pleasures, superior in respect of their specific quality or their source, that are desirable in themselves.

Let this suffice for a discussion of the current views about pleasure and pain.

We may ascertain the nature and quality of pleasure more clearly if we start again from the beginning.

Now the act of sight appears to be perfect at any moment of its duration; it does not require anything to supervene later in order to perfect its specific quality. But pleasure also appears to be a thing of this nature. For it is a whole, and one cannot at any moment put one's hand on a pleasure which will only exhibit its specific quality perfectly if its duration be prolonged.

It follows also that pleasure is not a form of motion. For every motion or process of change

οἰκοδομική, καὶ τελεία ὅταν ποιήσῃ οὗ ἐφίεται· ἢ ἐν ἅπαντι δὴ τῷ χρόνῳ ἢ τούτῳ. ἐν δὲ τοῖς μέρεσι τοῦ χρόνου πᾶσαι ἀτελεῖς, καὶ ἕτεραι τῷ εἴδει τῆς ὅλης καὶ ἀλλήλων. ἡ γὰρ τῶν λίθων σύνθεσις ἑτέρα τῆς τοῦ κίονος ῥαβδώσεως, καὶ αὗται τῆς τοῦ ναοῦ ποιήσεως· καὶ ἡ μὲν τοῦ ναοῦ τελεία (οὐδενὸς γὰρ ἐνδεὴς πρὸς τὸ προκείμενον), ἡ δὲ τῆς κρηπῖδος καὶ τοῦ τριγλύφου ἀτελής (μέρους γὰρ ἑκατέρα)· τῷ εἴδει οὖν διαφέρουσι, καὶ οὐκ ἔστιν ἐν ὁτῳοῦν χρόνῳ λαβεῖν κίνησιν τελείαν τῷ εἴδει, ἀλλ᾽ εἴπερ, ἐν τῷ ἅπαντι. ὁμοίως δὲ καὶ ἐπὶ βαδίσεως καὶ τῶν λοιπῶν· εἰ γάρ ἐστιν ἡ φορὰ κίνησις πόθεν ποῖ, καὶ ταύτης διαφοραὶ κατ᾽ εἴδη, πτῆσις βάδισις ἅλσις καὶ τὰ τοιαῦτα, οὐ μόνον δ᾽ οὕτως, ἀλλὰ καὶ ἐν αὐτῇ τῇ βαδίσει (τὸ γὰρ πόθεν ποῖ οὐ ταὐτὸν ἐν τῷ σταδίῳ καὶ ἐν τῷ μέρει, καὶ ἐν ἑτέρῳ

involves duration, and is a means to an end, for instance the process of building a house; and it is perfect when it has effected its end. Hence a motion is perfect either when viewed over the whole time of its duration, or at the moment when its end has been achieved. The several motions occupying portions of the time of the whole are imperfect, and different in kind from the whole and from each other. For instance, in building a temple the fitting together of the stones is a different process from the fluting of a column, and both are different from the construction of the temple as a whole; and whereas the building of the temple is a perfect process, for nothing more is required to achieve the end proposed, laying the foundation and constructing the triglyphs are imperfect processes, since each produces only a part of the design; they are therefore specifically different from the construction of the whole, and it is not possible to lay one's finger on a motion specifically perfect at any moment of the process of building, but only, if at all, in the whole of its duration.

μέρει καὶ ἑτέρῳ, οὐδὲ τὸ διεξιέναι τὴν γραμμὴν τήνδε κἀκείνην· οὐ μόνον γὰρ γραμμὴν διαπορεύεται, ἀλλὰ καὶ ἐν τόπῳ οὖσαν, ἐν ἑτέρῳ δ' αὕτη ἐκείνης) —δι' ἀκριβείας μὲν οὖν περὶ κινήσεως ἐν ἄλλοις εἴρηται, ἔοικε δ' οὐκ ἐν ἅπαντι χρόνῳ τελεία εἶναι, ἀλλ' αἱ πολλαὶ ἀτελεῖς, καὶ διαφέρουσαι τῷ εἴδει, εἴπερ τὸ πόθεν ποῖ εἰδοποιόν. τῆς ἡδονῆς δ' ἐν ὁτῳοῦν χρόνῳ τέλειον τὸ εἶδος. δῆλον οὖν ὡς ἕτεραί τ' ἂν εἶεν ἀλλήλων, καὶ τῶν ὅλων τι καὶ τελείων ἡ ἡδονή. δόξειε δ' ἂν τοῦτο καὶ ἐκ τοῦ μὴ ἐνδέχεσθαι κινεῖσθαι μὴ ἐν χρόνῳ, ἥδεσθαι δέ· τὸ γὰρ ἐν τῷ νῦν ὅλον τι. —ἐκ τούτων δὲ δῆλον καὶ ὅτι οὐ καλῶς λέγουσι κίνησιν ἢ γένεσιν εἶναι τῆς ἡδονῆς. οὐ γὰρ πάντων ταῦτα λέγεται, ἀλλὰ τῶν μεριστῶν καὶ μὴ ὅλων· οὐδὲ γὰρ ὁράσεώς ἐστι γένεσις οὐδὲ στιγμῆς οὐδὲ μονάδος (οὐδὲ τούτων

And the same is true of walking and the other forms of locomotion. For if locomotion is motion from one point in space to another, and if this is of different kinds, flying, walking, leaping and the like, and not only so, but if there are also differences in walking itself (for the terminal points of a race course are not the same as those of a portion of the course, nor are those of one portion the same as those of another; nor is traversing this line the same as traversing that one, for the runner does not merely travel along a certain line but travels along a line that is in a certain place, and this line is in a different place from that)—however, for a full treatment of the subject of motion I must refer to another work, but it appears that a motion is not perfect at every moment, but the many movements which make up the whole are imperfect; and different from each other in kind, inasmuch as the terminal points of a movement constitute a specific quality. The specific quality of pleasure on the contrary is perfect at any moment. It is clear therefore that pleasure is not the same as motion, and that it is a whole and something perfect.

οὐθὲν κίνησις οὐδὲ γένεσις) οὐδὲ δὴ ἡδονῆς· ὅλον γάρ τι.

Αἰσθήσεως δὲ πάσης πρὸς τὸ αἰσθητὸν ἐνεργούσης, τελείως δὲ τῆς εὖ διακειμένης πρὸς τὸ κάλλιστον τῶν ὑπὸ τὴν αἴσθησιν (τοιοῦτον γὰρ μάλιστ' εἶναι δοκεῖ ἡ τελεία ἐνέργεια· αὐτὴν δὲ λέγειν ἐνεργεῖν, ἢ ἐν ᾧ ἐστί, μηθὲν διαφερέτω), καθ' ἑκάστην δὴ βελτίστη ἐστὶν ἡ ἐνέργεια τοῦ ἄριστα διακειμένου πρὸς τὸ κράτιστον τῶν ὑπ' αὐτήν· αὕτη δ' ἂν τελειοτάτη εἴη καὶ ἡδίστη. κατὰ πᾶσαν γὰρ αἴσθησίν ἐστιν ἡδονή, ὁμοίως δὲ καὶ διάνοιαν καὶ θεωρίαν, ἡδίστη δ' ἡ τελειοτάτη, τελειοτάτη δ' ἡ τοῦ εὖ ἔχοντος πρὸς τὸ σπουδαιότατον τῶν ὑπ' αὐτήν· τελειοῖ δὲ τὴν ἐνέργειαν ἡ ἡδονή. οὐ τὸν αὐτὸν δὲ τρόπον ἥ τε ἡδονὴ τελειοῖ καὶ τὸ αἰσθητόν τε καὶ ἡ αἴσθησις, σπουδαῖα ὄντα, ὥσπερ οὐδ' ἡ ὑγίεια καὶ ὁ ἰατρὸς

This may also be inferred from the fact that a movement necessarily occupies a space of time, whereas a feeling of pleasure does not, for every moment of pleasurable consciousness is a perfect whole.

These considerations also show that it is a mistake to speak of pleasure as the result of a motion or of a process of generation. For we cannot so describe everything, but only such things as are divided into parts and are not wholes. Thus an act of sight, a geometrical point, an arithmetical unit are not the result of a process of generation (nor is any of them a motion or process). Pleasure therefore also is not the result of a motion or process; for pleasure is a whole.

Again, inasmuch as each of the senses acts in relation to its object, and acts perfectly when it is in good condition and directed to the finest of the and objects that belong to it (for this seems to be the best description of perfect activity, it being assumed to make no difference whether it be the sense itself that acts or the organ in which the sense resides), it follows that the activity of any of the

ὁμοίως αἴτιά ἐστι τοῦ ὑγιαίνειν. (καθ' ἑκάστην δ' αἴσθησιν ὅτι γίνεται ἡδονή, δῆλον· φαμὲν γὰρ ὁράματα καὶ ἀκούσματα εἶναι ἡδέα· δῆλον δὲ καὶ ὅτι μάλιστα, ἐπειδὰν ἥ τε αἴσθησις ᾖ κρατίστη καὶ πρὸς τοιοῦτον ἐνεργῇ· τοιούτων δ' ὄντων τοῦ τε αἰσθητοῦ καὶ τοῦ αἰσθανομένου, ἀεὶ ἔσται ἡδονὴ ὑπάρχοντός γε τοῦ τε ποιήσοντος καὶ τοῦ πεισομένου.) τελειοῖ δὲ τὴν ἐνέργειαν ἡ ἡδονὴ οὐχ ὡς ἡ ἕξις ἐνυπάρχουσα, ἀλλ' ὡς ἐπιγιγνόμενόν τι τέλος, οἷον τοῖς ἀκμαίοις ἡ ὥρα. ἕως ἂν οὖν τό τε νοητὸν ἢ αἰσθητὸν ᾖ οἷον δεῖ καὶ τὸ κρῖνον ἢ θεωροῦν, ἔσται ἐν τῇ ἐνεργείᾳ ἡ ἡδονή· ὁμοίων γὰρ ὄντων καὶ πρὸς ἄλληλα τὸν αὐτὸν τρόπον ἐχόντων τοῦ τε παθητικοῦ καὶ τοῦ ποιητικοῦ ταὐτὸ πέφυκε γίνεσθαι. —πῶς οὖν οὐδεὶς συνεχῶς ἥδεται; ἢ κάμνει; πάντα γὰρ τὰ ἀνθρώπεια ἀδυνατεῖ συνεχῶς

senses is at its best when the sense-organ being in the best condition is directed to the best of its objects; and this activity will be the most perfect and the pleasantest. For each sense has a corresponding pleasure, as also have thought and speculation, and its activity is pleasantest when it is most perfect, and most perfect when the organ is in good condition and when it is directed to the most excellent of its objects; and the pleasure perfects the activity. The pleasure does not however perfect the activity in the same way as the object perceived and the sensory faculty, if good, perfect it; just as health and the physician are not in the same way the cause of being healthy.

(It is clear that each of the senses is accompanied by pleasure, since we apply the term pleasant to sights and sounds; and it is also clear that the pleasure is greatest when the sensory faculty is both in the best condition and acting in relation to the best object; and given excellence in the perceived object and the percipient organ, there will always be pleasure when an object to cause it and a subject to feel it are both present.)

ἐνεργεῖν· οὐ γίνεται οὖν οὐδ' ἡδονή, ἕπεται γὰρ τῇ ἐνεργείᾳ. ἔνια δὲ τέρπει καινὰ ὄντα, ὕστερον δὲ οὐχ ὁμοίως διὰ ταὐτό· τὸ μὲν γὰρ πρῶτον παρακέκληται ἡ διάνοια καὶ διατεταμένως περὶ αὐτὰ ἐνεργεῖ, ὥσπερ κατὰ τὴν ὄψιν οἱ ἐμβλέποντες, μετέπειτα δ' οὐ τοιαύτη ἡ ἐνέργεια ἀλλὰ παρημελημένη· διὸ καὶ ἡ ἡδονὴ ἀμαυροῦται. —ὀρέγεσθαι δὲ τῆς ἡδονῆς οἰηθείη τις ἂν ἅπαντας, ὅτι καὶ τοῦ ζῆν ἅπαντες ἐφίενται· ἡ δὲ ζωὴ ἐνέργειά τις ἐστι, καὶ ἕκαστος περὶ ταῦτα καὶ τούτοις ἐνεργεῖ ἃ καὶ μάλιστ' ἀγαπᾷ, οἷον ὁ μὲν μουσικὸς τῇ ἀκοῇ περὶ τὰ μέλη, ὁ δὲ φιλομαθὴς τῇ διανοίᾳ περὶ τὰ θεωρήματα, οὕτω δὲ καὶ τῶν λοιπῶν ἕκαστος. ἡ δ' ἡδονὴ τελειοῖ τὰς ἐνεργείας, καὶ τὸ ζῆν δή, οὗ ὀρέγονται. εὐλόγως οὖν καὶ τῆς ἡδονῆς ἐφίενται· τελειοῖ γὰρ ἑκάστῳ τὸ ζῆν, αἱρετὸν ὄν. πότερον δὲ διὰ τὴν

But the pleasure perfects the activity, not as the fixed disposition does, by being already present in the agent, but as a supervening perfection, like the bloom of health in the young and vigorous.

So long therefore as both object thought of or perceived, and subject discerning or judging, are such as they should be, there will be pleasure in the activity; since while both the passive and the active parties to a relationship remain the same in themselves and unaltered in their relation to one another, the same result is naturally produced.

How is it then that no one can feel pleasure continuously? Perhaps it is due to fatigue, since no human faculty is capable of uninterrupted activity, and therefore pleasure also is not continuous, because it accompanies the activity of the faculties. It is for the same reason that some things please us when new, but cease to give so much pleasure later; this is because at first the mind is stimulated, and acts vigorously in regard to the object, as in the case of sight when we look at something intently; but afterwards the activity is less vigorous and our attention relaxes, and consequently the pleasure also fades.

ἡδονὴν τὸ ζῆν αἱρούμεθα ἢ διὰ τὸ ζῆν τὴν ἡδονήν, ἀφείσθω ἐν τῷ παρόντι. συνεζεῦχθαι μὲν γὰρ ταῦτα φαίνεται καὶ χωρισμὸν οὐ δέχεσθαι· ἄνευ τε γὰρ ἐνεργείας οὐ γίνεται ἡδονή, πᾶσάν τε ἐνέργειαν τελειοῖ ἡ ἡδονή.

V Ὅθεν δοκοῦσι καὶ τῷ εἴδει διαφέρειν· τὰ γὰρ ἕτερα τῷ εἴδει ὑφ' ἑτέρων οἰόμεθα τελειοῦσθαι. οὕτω γὰρ φαίνεται καὶ τὰ φυσικὰ καὶ τὰ ὑπὸ τέχνης, οἷον ζῷα καὶ δένδρα καὶ γραφὴ καὶ ἄγαλμα καὶ οἰκία

It might be held that all men seek to obtain pleasure, because all men desire life. Life is a form of activity, and each man exercises his activity upon those objects and with those faculties which he likes the most: for example, the musician exercises his sense of hearing upon musical tunes, the student his intellect upon problems of philosophy, and so on. And the pleasure of these activities perfects the activities, and therefore perfects life, which all men seek. Men have good reason therefore to pursue pleasure, since it perfects for each his life, which is a desirable thing. The question whether we desire life for the sake of pleasure or pleasure for the sake of life, need not be raised for the present. In any case they appear to be inseparably united; for there is no pleasure without activity, and also no perfect activity without its pleasure.

This moreover is the ground for believing that pleasures vary in specific quality. For we feel that different kinds of things must have a different sort of perfection. We see this to be so with natural organisms and the productions of art, such as animals, trees, a picture, a statue, a house, a piece of

καὶ σκεῦος· ὁμοίως δὲ καὶ τὰς ἐνεργείας τὰς διαφερούσας τῷ εἴδει ὑπὸ διαφερόντων εἴδει τελειοῦσθαι. διαφέρουσι δ' αἱ τῆς διανοίας τῶν κατὰ τὰς αἰσθήσεις καὶ αὐταὶ ἀλλήλων κατ' εἶδος· καὶ αἱ τελειοῦσαι δὴ ἡδοναί. —φανείη δ' ἂν τοῦτο καὶ ἐκ τοῦ συνῳκειῶσθαι τῶν ἡδονῶν ἑκάστην τῇ ἐνεργείᾳ ἣν τελειοῖ. συναύξει γὰρ τὴν ἐνέργειαν ἡ οἰκεία ἡδονή· μᾶλλον γὰρ ἕκαστα κρίνουσι καὶ ἐξακριβοῦσιν οἱ μεθ' ἡδονῆς ἐνεργοῦντες, οἷον γεωμετρικοὶ γίνονται οἱ χαίροντες τῷ γεωμετρεῖν, καὶ κατανοοῦσιν ἕκαστα μᾶλλον, ὁμοίως δὲ καὶ οἱ φιλόμουσοι καὶ φιλοικοδόμοι καὶ τῶν ἄλλων ἕκαστοι ἐπιδιδόασιν εἰς τὸ οἰκεῖον ἔργον χαίροντες αὐτῷ. συναύξουσι δὴ αἱ ἡδοναί, τὰ δὲ συναύξοντα οἰκεῖα. τοῖς ἑτέροις δὲ τῷ εἴδει καὶ τὰ οἰκεῖα ἕτερα τῷ εἴδει. —ἔτι δὲ μᾶλλον τοῦτ' ἂν φανείη ἐκ τοῦ τὰς ἀφ' ἑτέρων

furniture. Similarly we think that that which perfects one kind of activity must differ in kind from that which perfects another kind. Now the activities of the intellect differ from those of the senses, and from one another, in kind: so also therefore do the pleasures that perfect them.

This may also be seen from the affinity which exists between the various pleasures and the activities which they perfect. For an activity is augmented by the pleasure that belongs to it; since those who work with pleasure always work with more discernment and with greater accuracy—for instance, students who are fond of geometry become proficient in it, and grasp its various problems better, and similarly lovers of music, architecture or the other arts make progress in their favorite pursuit because they enjoy it. An activity then is augmented by its pleasure; and that which augments a thing must be akin to it. But things that are akin to things of different kinds must themselves differ in kind. A still clearer proof may be drawn from the hindrance that activities receive from the pleasure derived from other activities. For

ἡδονὰς ἐμποδίους ταῖς ἐνεργείαις εἶναι. οἱ γὰρ φίλαυλοι ἀδυνατοῦσι τοῖς λόγοις προσέχειν, ἐὰν κατακούσωσιν αὐλοῦντος, μᾶλλον χαίροντες αὐλητικῇ τῆς παρούσης ἐνεργείας· ἡ κατὰ τὴν αὐλητικὴν οὖν ἡδονὴ τὴν περὶ τὸν λόγον ἐνέργειαν φθείρει. ὁμοίως δὲ τοῦτο καὶ ἐπὶ τῶν ἄλλων συμβαίνει, ὅταν ἅμα περὶ δύο ἐνεργῇ· ἡ γὰρ ἡδίων τὴν ἑτέραν ἐκκρούει, κἂν πολὺ διαφέρῃ κατὰ τὴν ἡδονήν, μᾶλλον, ὥστε μηδ' ἐνεργεῖν κατὰ τὴν ἑτέραν. διὸ χαίροντες ὁτῳοῦν σφόδρα οὐ πάνυ δρῶμεν ἕτερον· καὶ ἄλλα ποιοῦμεν ἄλλοις ἠρέμα ἀρεσκόμενοι, οἷον καὶ ἐν τοῖς θεάτροις οἱ τραγηματίζοντες, ὅταν φαῦλοι οἱ ἀγωνιζόμενοι ὦσι, τότε μάλιστ' αὐτὸ δρῶσιν. ἐπεὶ δ' ἡ μὲν οἰκεία ἡδονὴ ἐξακριβοῖ τὰς ἐνεργείας καὶ χρονιωτέρας καὶ βελτίους ποιεῖ, αἱ δ' ἀλλότριαι λυμαίνονται, δῆλον ὡς πολὺ διεστᾶσιν· σχεδὸν γὰρ αἱ ἀλλό-

instance, persons fond of the flute cannot give their attention to a philosophical discussion when they overhear someone playing the flute, because they enjoy music more than the activity in which they are engaged; therefore the pleasure afforded by the music of the flute impairs the activity of study. The same thing occurs in other cases when a man tries to do two things at once; the pleasanter activity drives out the other, the more so if it is much more pleasant, until the other activity ceases altogether. Hence, when we enjoy something very much, we can hardly do anything else; and when we find a thing only mildly agreeable, we turn to some other occupation; for instance, people who eat sweets at the theater do so especially when the acting is bad. And since our activities are sharpened, prolonged and improved by their own pleasure, and impaired by the pleasures of other activities, it is clear that pleasures differ widely from each other. In fact alien pleasures have almost the same effect on the activities as their own pains; since, when an activity causes pain, this pain destroys it, for instance, if a person finds writing or doing sums unpleasant

τριαι ἡδοναὶ ποιοῦσιν ὅπερ αἱ οἰκεῖαι λῦπαι· φθείρουσι γὰρ τὰς ἐνεργείας αἱ οἰκεῖαι λῦπαι, οἷον εἴ τῳ τὸ γράφειν ἀηδὲς καὶ ἐπίλυπον ἢ τὸ λογίζεσθαι· ὃ μὲν γὰρ οὐ γράφει, ὃ δ' οὐ λογίζεται, λυπηρᾶς οὔσης τῆς ἐνεργείας. συμβαίνει δὴ περὶ τὰς ἐνεργείας τοὐναντίον ἀπὸ τῶν οἰκείων ἡδονῶν τε καὶ λυπῶν· οἰκεῖαι δ' εἰσὶν αἱ ἐπὶ τῇ ἐνεργείᾳ καθ' αὑτὴν γινόμεναι. αἱ δ' ἀλλότριαι ἡδοναὶ εἴρηται ὅτι παραπλήσιόν τι τῇ λύπῃ ποιοῦσιν· φθείρουσι γάρ, πλὴν οὐχ ὁμοίως.

Διαφερουσῶν δὲ τῶν ἐνεργειῶν ἐπιεικείᾳ καὶ φαυλότητι, καὶ τῶν μὲν αἱρετῶν οὐσῶν, τῶν δὲ φευκτῶν, τῶν δ' οὐδετέρων, ὁμοίως ἔχουσι καὶ αἱ ἡδοναί· καθ' ἑκάστην γὰρ ἐνέργειαν οἰκεία ἡδονή ἐστιν. ἡ μὲν οὖν τῇ σπουδαίᾳ οἰκεία ἐπιεικής, ἡ δὲ τῇ φαύλῃ μοχθηρά· καὶ γὰρ αἱ ἐπιθυμίαι τῶν μὲν καλῶν ἐπαινεταί, τῶν

and irksome; for he stops writing or doing sums, because the activity is painful. Activities then are affected in opposite ways by the pleasures and the pains that belong to them, that is to say, those that are intrinsically due to their exercise. Alien pleasures, as has been said, have very much the same effect as pain, for they destroy an activity, only not to the same degree.

Again, since activities differ in moral value, and some are to be adopted, others to be avoided, and others again are neutral, the same is true also of their pleasures: for each activity has a pleasure of its own. Thus the pleasure of a good activity is morally good, that of a bad one morally bad; for even desires for noble things are praised and desires for base things blamed; but the pleasures contained in our activities are more intimately connected with them than the appetites which prompt them, for the appetite is both separate in time and distinct in its nature from the activity, whereas the pleasure is closely linked to the activity, indeed so inseparable from it as to raise a doubt whether the activity is not the same thing as the

δ' αἰσχρῶν ψεκταί· οἰκειότεραι δὲ ταῖς ἐνεργείαις αἱ ἐν αὐταῖς ἡδοναὶ τῶν ὀρέξεων· αἱ μὲν γὰρ διωρισμέναι εἰσὶ καὶ τοῖς χρόνοις καὶ τῇ φύσει, αἱ δὲ σύνεγγυς ταῖς ἐνεργείαις, καὶ ἀδιόριστοι οὕτως ὥστ' ἔχειν ἀμφισβήτησιν εἰ ταὐτόν ἐστιν ἡ ἐνέργεια τῇ ἡδονῇ. οὐ μὴν ἔοικέ γε ἡ ἡδονὴ διάνοια εἶναι οὐδ' αἴσθησις (ἄτοπον γάρ), ἀλλὰ διὰ τὸ μὴ χωρίζεσθαι φαίνεταί τισι ταὐτόν. ὥσπερ οὖν αἱ ἐνέργειαι ἕτεραι, καὶ αἱ ἡδοναί. διαφέρει δὲ ἡ ὄψις ἁφῆς καθαρειότητι, καὶ ἀκοὴ καὶ ὄσφρησις γεύσεως· ὁμοίως δὴ διαφέρουσι καὶ αἱ ἡδοναί, καὶ τούτων αἱ περὶ τὴν διάνοιαν, καὶ ἑκάτεραι ἀλλήλων. δοκεῖ δ' εἶναι ἑκάστῳ ζῴῳ καὶ ἡδονὴ οἰκεία, ὥσπερ καὶ ἔργον· ἡ γὰρ κατὰ τὴν ἐνέργειαν. καὶ ἐφ' ἑκάστῳ δὲ θεωροῦντι τοῦτ' ἂν φανείη· ἑτέρα γὰρ ἵππου ἡδονὴ καὶ κυνὸς καὶ ἀνθρώπου, καθάπερ Ἡράκλειτός φησιν

pleasure. However, we must not regard pleasure as really being a thought or a sensation—indeed this is absurd, though because they are inseparable they seem to some people to be the same.

As then activities are diverse, so also are their pleasures. Sight excels touch in purity, and hearing and smell excel taste; and similarly the pleasures of the intellect excel in purity the pleasures of sensation, while the pleasures of either class differ among themselves in purity.

And it is thought that every animal has its own special pleasure, just as it has its own special function: namely, the pleasure of exercising that function. This will also appear if we consider the different animals one by one: the horse, the dog, man, have different pleasures—as Heracleitus says, an ass would prefer chaff to gold, since to asses food gives more pleasure than gold. Different species therefore have different kinds of pleasures. On the other hand it might be supposed that there is no variety among the pleasures of the same species. But as a matter of fact in the human species at all events there is a great diversity of pleasures. The

ὄνον σύρματ' ἂν ἑλέσθαι μᾶλλον ἢ χρυσόν· ἥδιον γὰρ χρυσοῦ τροφὴ ὄνοις. αἱ μὲν οὖν τῶν ἑτέρων τῷ εἴδει διαφέρουσιν εἴδει, τὰς δὲ τῶν αὐτῶν ἀδιαφόρους εὔλογον εἶναι· διαλλάττουσι δ' οὐ μικρὸν ἐπί γε τῶν ἀνθρώπων· τὰ γὰρ αὐτὰ τοὺς μὲν τέρπει, τοὺς δὲ λυπεῖ, καὶ τοῖς μὲν λυπηρὰ καὶ μισητά ἐστι, τοῖς δὲ ἡδέα καὶ φιλητά. καὶ ἐπὶ γλυκέων δὲ τοῦτο συμβαίνει· οὐ γὰρ τὰ αὐτὰ δοκεῖ τῷ πυρέττοντι καὶ τῷ ὑγιαίνοντι, οὐδὲ θερμὸν εἶναι τῷ ἀσθενεῖ καὶ τῷ εὐεκτικῷ. ὁμοίως δὲ τοῦτο καὶ ἐφ' ἑτέρων συμβαίνει. δοκεῖ δ' ἐν ἅπασι τοῖς τοιούτοις εἶναι τὸ φαινόμενον τῷ σπουδαίῳ. εἰ δὲ τοῦτο καλῶς λέγεται, καθάπερ δοκεῖ, καὶ ἔστιν ἑκάστου μέτρον ἡ ἀρετὴ καὶ ἀγαθός, ᾗ τοιοῦτος, καὶ ἡδοναὶ εἶεν ἂν αἱ τούτῳ φαινόμεναι καὶ ἡδέα οἷς οὗτος χαίρει. τὰ δὲ τούτῳ δυσχερῆ εἴ τῳ φαίνεται ἡδέα, οὐδὲν θαυμαστόν·

same things delight some men and annoy others, and things painful and disgusting to some are pleasant and attractive to others. This also holds good of things sweet to the taste: the same things do not taste sweet to a man in a fever as to one in good health; nor does the same temperature feel warm to an invalid and to a person of robust constitution. The same holds good of other things as well.

But we hold that in all such cases the thing really is what it appears to be to the good man. And if this rule is sound, as it is generally held to be, and if the standard of everything is goodness, or the good man, qua good, then the things that seem to him to be pleasures are pleasures, and the things he enjoys are pleasant. Nor need it cause surprise that things disagreeable to the good man should seem pleasant to some men; for mankind is liable to many corruptions and diseases, and the things in question are not really pleasant, but only pleasant to these particular persons, who are in a condition to think them so.

It is therefore clear that we must pronounce the admittedly disgraceful pleasures not to be pleasures at all, except to the depraved.

πολλαὶ γὰρ φθοραὶ καὶ λῦμαι ἀνθρώπων γίνονται· ἡδέα δ' οὐκ ἔστιν, ἀλλ' ἢ τούτοις καὶ οὕτω διακειμένοις. τὰς μὲν οὖν ὁμολογουμένως αἰσχρὰς δῆλον ὡς οὐ φατέον ἡδονὰς εἶναι, πλὴν τοῖς διεφθαρμένοις· τῶν δ' ἐπιεικῶν εἶναι δοκουσῶν ποίαν ἢ τίνα φατέον τοῦ ἀνθρώπου εἶναι; ἢ ἐκ τῶν ἐνεργειῶν δῆλον; ταύταις γὰρ ἕπονται αἱ ἡδοναί. εἴτ' οὖν μία ἐστὶν εἴτε πλείους αἱ τοῦ τελείου καὶ μακαρίου ἀνδρός, αἱ ταύτας τελειοῦσαι ἡδοναὶ κυρίως λέγοιντ' ἂν ἀνθρώπου ἡδοναὶ εἶναι, αἱ δὲ λοιπαὶ δευτέρως καὶ πολλοστῶς, ὥσπερ αἱ ἐνέργειαι.

VI Εἰρημένων δὲ τῶν περὶ τὰς ἀρετάς τε καὶ φιλίας καὶ ἡδονάς, λοιπὸν περὶ εὐδαιμονίας τύπῳ διελθεῖν, ἐπειδὴ τέλος αὐτὴν τίθεμεν τῶν ἀνθρωπίνων. ἀναλαβοῦσι δὲ τὰ προειρημένα συντομώτερος ἂν εἴη ὁ

But among the pleasures considered respectable, which class of pleasures or which particular pleasure is to be deemed the distinctively human pleasure? Perhaps this will be clear from a consideration of man's activities. For pleasures correspond to the activities to which they belong; it is therefore that pleasure, or those pleasures, by which the activity, or the activities, of the perfect and supremely happy man are perfected, that must be pronounced human in the fullest sense. The other pleasures are so only in a secondary or some lower degree, like the activities to which they belong.

Having now discussed the various kinds of Virtue, of Friendship and of Pleasure, it remains for us to treat in outline of Happiness, inasmuch as we count this to be the End of human life. But it will shorten the discussion if we recapitulate what has been said already.

Now we stated that happiness is not a certain disposition of character; since if it were it might be possessed by a man who passed the whole of his chosen life asleep, living the life of a vegetable, or by one who was plunged in the deepest misfortune. If

λόγος. εἴπομεν δὴ ὅτι οὐκ ἔστιν ἕξις· καὶ γὰρ τῷ καθεύδοντι διὰ βίου ὑπάρχοι ἄν, φυτοῦ ζῶντι βίον, καὶ τῷ δυστυχοῦντι τὰ μέγιστα. εἰ δὴ ταῦτα μὴ ἀρέσκει, ἀλλὰ μᾶλλον εἰς ἐνέργειάν τινα θετέον, καθάπερ ἐν τοῖς πρότερον εἴρηται, τῶν δ᾽ ἐνεργειῶν αἱ μέν εἰσιν ἀναγκαῖαι καὶ δι᾽ ἕτερα αἱρεταί, αἱ δὲ καθ᾽ αὑτάς, δῆλον ὅτι τὴν εὐδαιμονίαν τῶν καθ᾽ αὑτὰς αἱρετῶν τινα θετέον καὶ οὐ τῶν δι᾽ ἄλλο· οὐδενὸς γὰρ ἐνδεὴς ἡ εὐδαιμονία ἀλλ᾽ αὐτάρκης. καθ᾽ αὑτὰς δ᾽ εἰσὶν αἱρεταὶ ἀφ᾽ ὧν μηδὲν ἐπιζητεῖται παρὰ τὴν ἐνέργειαν. τοιαῦται δ᾽ εἶναι δοκοῦσιν αἱ κατ᾽ ἀρετὴν πράξεις· τὰ γὰρ καλὰ καὶ σπουδαῖα πράττειν τῶν δι᾽ αὑτὰ αἱρετῶν. καὶ τῶν παιδιῶν δὲ αἱ ἡδεῖαι· οὐ γὰρ δι᾽ ἕτερα αὐτὰς αἱροῦνται· βλάπτονται γὰρ ἀπ᾽ αὐτῶν μᾶλλον ἢ ὠφελοῦνται, ἀμελοῦντες τῶν σωμάτων καὶ τῆς κτήσεως. καταφεύγουσι δ᾽ ἐπὶ τὰς τοι-

then we reject this as unsatisfactory, and feel bound to class happiness rather as some form of activity, as has been said in the earlier part of this treatise, and if activities are of two kinds, some merely necessary means and desirable only for the sake of something else, others desirable in themselves, it is clear that happiness is to be classed among activities desirable in themselves, and not among those desirable as a means to something else; since happiness lacks nothing, and is self-sufficient.

But those activities are desirable in themselves which do not aim at any result beyond the mere exercise of the activity. Now this is felt to be the nature of actions in conformity with virtue; for to do noble and virtuous deeds is a thing desirable for its own sake.

But agreeable amusements also are desirable for not their own sake; we do not pursue them as a means to something else, for as a matter of fact they are more often harmful than beneficial, causing men to neglect their health and their estates. Yet persons whom the world counts happy usually have recourse to such pastimes; and this is why

αὑτὰς διαγωγὰς τῶν εὐδαιμονιζομένων οἱ πολλοί, διὸ παρὰ τοῖς τυράννοις εὐδοκιμοῦσιν οἱ ἐν ταῖς τοιαύταις διαγωγαῖς εὐτράπελοι· ὧν γὰρ ἐφίενται, ἐν τούτοις παρέχουσι σφᾶς αὐτοὺς ἡδεῖς, δέονται δὲ τοιούτων. δοκεῖ μὲν οὖν εὐδαιμονικὰ ταῦτα εἶναι διὰ τὸ τοὺς ἐν δυναστείαις ἐν τούτοις ἀποσχολάζειν, οὐδὲν δὲ ἴσως σημεῖον οἱ τοιοῦτοί εἰσιν· οὐ γὰρ ἐν τῷ δυναστεύειν ἡ ἀρετὴ οὐδ' ὁ νοῦς, ἀφ' ὧν αἱ σπουδαῖαι ἐνέργειαι· οὐδ' εἰ ἄγευστοι οὗτοι ὄντες ἡδονῆς εἰλικρινοῦς καὶ ἐλευθερίου ἐπὶ τὰς σωματικὰς καταφεύγουσιν, διὰ τοῦτο ταύτας οἰητέον αἱρετωτέρας εἶναι. καὶ γὰρ οἱ παῖδες τὰ παρ' αὐτοῖς τιμώμενα κράτιστα οἴονται εἶναι· εὔλογον δή, ὥσπερ παισὶ καὶ ἀνδράσιν ἕτερα φαίνεται τίμια, οὕτω καὶ φαύλοις καὶ ἐπιεικέσιν. καθάπερ οὖν πολλάκις εἴρηται, καὶ τίμια καὶ ἡδέα ἐστὶ τὰ τῷ σπουδαίῳ τοιαῦτα

adepts in such pastimes stand in high favor with princes, because they make themselves agreeable in supplying what their patrons desire, and what they want is amusement. So it is supposed that amusements are a component part of happiness, because princes and potentates devote their leisure to them.

But (i) perhaps princes and potentates are not good evidence. Virtue and intelligence, which are the sources of man's higher activities, do not depend on the possession of power; and if these persons, having no taste fo pure and liberal pleasure, have recourse to the pleasures of the body, we must not on that account suppose that bodily pleasures are the more desirable. Children imagine that the things they themselves value are actually the best; it is not surprising therefore that, as children and grown men have different standards of value, so also should the worthless and the virtuous. Therefore, as has repeatedly been said, those things are actually valuable and pleasant which appear so to the good man; but each man thinks that activity most desirable which suits his particular disposition, and there fore the good a man

ὄντα· ἑκάστῳ δ' ἡ κατὰ τὴν οἰκείαν ἕξιν αἱρετωτάτη ἐνέργεια, καὶ τῷ σπουδαίῳ δὴ ἡ κατὰ τὴν ἀρετήν. οὐκ ἐν παιδιᾷ ἄρα ἡ εὐδαιμονία. καὶ γὰρ ἄτοπον τὸ τέλος εἶναι παιδιάν, καὶ πραγματεύεσθαι καὶ κακοπαθεῖν τὸν βίον ἅπαντα τοῦ παίζειν χάριν. ἅπαντα γὰρ ὡς εἰπεῖν ἑτέρου ἕνεκα αἱρούμεθα πλὴν τῆς εὐδαιμονίας· τέλος γὰρ αὕτη· σπουδάζειν δὲ καὶ πονεῖν παιδιᾶς χάριν ἠλίθιον φαίνεται καὶ λίαν παιδικόν· παίζειν δ' ὅπως σπουδάζῃ, κατ' Ἀνάχαρσιν, ὀρθῶς ἔχειν δοκεῖ· ἀναπαύσει γὰρ ἔοικεν ἡ παιδιά· ἀδυνατοῦντες δὲ συνεχῶς πονεῖν ἀναπαύσεως δέονται· οὐ δὴ τέλος ἡ ἀνάπαυσις· γίνεται γὰρ ἕνεκα τῆς ἐνεργείας. δοκεῖ δ' εὐδαίμων βίος ὁ κατ' ἀρετὴν εἶναι· οὗτος δὲ μετὰ σπουδῆς, ἀλλ' οὐκ ἐν παιδιᾷ. βελτίω τε λέγομεν τὰ σπουδαῖα τῶν γελοίων καὶ τῶν μετὰ παιδιᾶς, καὶ τοῦ βελτίονος ἀεὶ καὶ μορίου καὶ

thinks virtuous activity most desirable. It follows therefore that happiness is not to be found in amusements.

(ii) Indeed it would be strange that amusement should be our End—that we should toil and moil all our life long in order that we may amuse ourselves. For virtually every object we adopt is pursued as a means to something else, excepting happiness, which is an end in itself; to make amusement the object of our serious pursuits and our work seems foolish and childish to excess: Anacharsis's motto, Play in order that you may work, is felt to be the right rule. For amusement is a form of rest; but we need rest because we are not able to go on working without a break, and therefore it is not an end, since we take it as a means to further activity.

(iii) And the life that conforms with virtue is thought to be a happy life; but virtuous life involves serious purpose, and does not consist in amusement.

(iv) Also we pronounce serious things to be superior to things that are funny and amusing; and the nobler a faculty or a person is, the more serious,

ἀνθρώπου σπουδαιοτέραν τὴν ἐνέργειαν·
ἡ δὴ τοῦ βελτίονος κρείττων, καὶ εὐδαιμο-
νικωτέρα ἤδη. ἀπολαύσειέ τ' ἂν τῶν σω-
ματικῶν ἡδονῶν ὁ τυχὼν καὶ ἀνδράποδον
οὐχ ἧττον τοῦ ἀρίστου· εὐδαιμονίας δ'
οὐδεὶς ἀνδραπόδῳ μεταδίδωσιν, εἰ μὴ καὶ
βίου. οὐκ ἄρ' ἐν ταῖς τοιαύταις διαγωγαῖς
ἡ εὐδαιμονία, ἀλλ' ἐν ταῖς κατ' ἀρετὴν
ἐνεργείαις, καθάπερ καὶ πρότερον εἴρηται.

VII Εἰ δ' ἐστὶν ἡ εὐδαιμονία κατ' ἀρετὴν
ἐνέργεια, εὔλογον κατὰ τὴν κρατίστην·
αὕτη δ' ἂν εἴη τοῦ ἀρίστου. εἴτε δὴ νοῦς
τοῦτο εἴτε ἄλλο τι, ὃ δὴ κατὰ φύσιν δοκεῖ
ἄρχειν καὶ ἡγεῖσθαι καὶ ἔννοιαν ἔχειν
περὶ καλῶν καὶ θείων, εἴτε θεῖον ὂν καὶ
αὐτὸ εἴτε τῶν ἐν ἡμῖν τὸ θειότατον, ἡ
τούτου ἐνέργεια κατὰ τὴν οἰκείαν ἀρετὴν
εἴη ἂν ἡ τελεία εὐδαιμονία· ὅτι δ' ἐστὶ
θεωρητική, εἴρηται. ὁμολογούμενον δὲ
τοῦτ' ἂν δόξειεν εἶναι καὶ τοῖς πρότερον

we think, are their activities; therefore, the activity of the nobler faculty or person is itself superior, and therefore more productive of happiness.

(v) Also anybody can enjoy the pleasures of the body, a slave no less than the noblest of mankind; but no one allows a slave any measure of happiness, any more than a life of his own. Therefore happiness does not consist in pastimes and amusements, but in activities in accordance with virtue, as has been said already.

But if happiness consists in activity in accordance with virtue, it is reasonable that it should be activity in accordance with the highest virtue; and this will be the virtue of the best part of us. Whether then this be the intellect, or whatever else it be that is thought to rule and lead us by nature, and to have cognizance of what is noble and divine, either as being itself also actually divine, or as being relatively the divinest part of us, it is the activity of this part of us in accordance with the virtue proper to it that will constitute perfect happiness; and it has been stated already that this activity is the activity of contemplation.

καὶ τῷ ἀληθεῖ. κρατίστη τε γὰρ αὕτη ἐστὶν ἡ ἐνέργεια (καὶ γὰρ ὁ νοῦς τῶν ἐν ἡμῖν, καὶ τῶν γνωστῶν, περὶ ἃ ὁ νοῦς)· ἔτι δὲ συνεχεστάτη, θεωρεῖν [τε] γὰρ δυνάμεθα συνεχῶς μᾶλλον ἢ πράττειν ὁτιοῦν. οἰόμεθά τε δεῖν ἡδονὴν παραμεμῖχθαι τῇ εὐδαιμονίᾳ, ἡδίστη δὲ τῶν κατ' ἀρετὴν ἐνεργειῶν ἡ κατὰ τὴν σοφίαν ὁμολογουμένως ἐστίν· δοκεῖ γοῦν ἡ φιλοσοφία θαυμαστὰς ἡδονὰς ἔχειν καθαρειότητι καὶ τῷ βεβαίῳ, εὔλογον δὲ τοῖς εἰδόσι τῶν ζητούντων ἡδίω τὴν διαγωγὴν εἶναι. ἥ τε λεγομένη αὐτάρκεια περὶ τὴν θεωρητικὴν μάλιστ' ἂν εἴη· τῶν μὲν γὰρ πρὸς τὸ ζῆν ἀναγκαίων καὶ σοφὸς καὶ δίκαιος καὶ οἱ λοιποὶ δέονται, τοῖς δὲ τοιούτοις ἱκανῶς κεχορηγημένων ὁ μὲν δίκαιος δεῖται πρὸς οὓς δικαιοπραγήσει καὶ μεθ' ὧν, ὁμοίως δὲ καὶ ὁ σώφρων καὶ ὁ ἀνδρεῖος καὶ τῶν ἄλλων ἕκαστος, ὁ δὲ

And that happiness consists in contemplation may be accepted as agreeing both with the results already reached and with the truth. For contemplation is at once the highest form of activity (since the intellect is the highest thing in us, and the objects with which the intellect deals are the highest things that can be known), and also it is the most continuous, for we can reflect more continuously than we can carry on any form of action. And again we suppose that happiness must contain an element of pleasure; now activity in accordance with wisdom is admittedly the most pleasant of the activities in accordance with virtue: at all events it is held that philosophy or the pursuit of wisdom contains pleasures of marvellous purity and permanence, and it is reasonable to suppose that the enjoyment of knowledge is a still pleasanter occupation than the pursuit of it. Also the activity of contemplation will be found to possess in the highest degree the quality that is termed self-sufficiency; for while it is true that the wise man equally with the just man and the rest requires the necessaries of life, yet, these being adequately supplied, whereas the just

σοφὸς καὶ καθ' αὑτὸν ὢν δύναται θεωρεῖν, καὶ ὅσῳ ἂν σοφώτερος ᾖ, μᾶλλον· βέλτιον δ' ἴσως συνεργοὺς ἔχων, ἀλλ' ὅμως αὐταρκέστατος. δόξαι τ' ἂν αὐτὴ μόνη δι' αὑτὴν ἀγαπᾶσθαι· οὐδὲν γὰρ ἀπ' αὐτῆς γίνεται παρὰ τὸ θεωρῆσαι, ἀπὸ δὲ τῶν πρακτικῶν ἢ πλεῖον ἢ ἔλαττον περιποιούμεθα παρὰ τὴν πρᾶξιν. δοκεῖ τε ἡ εὐδαιμονία ἐν τῇ σχολῇ εἶναι· ἀσχολούμεθα γὰρ ἵνα σχολάζωμεν, καὶ πολεμοῦμεν ἵν' εἰρήνην ἄγωμεν. τῶν μὲν οὖν πρακτικῶν ἀρετῶν ἐν τοῖς πολιτικοῖς ἢ ἐν τοῖς πολεμικοῖς ἡ ἐνέργεια· αἱ δὲ περὶ ταῦτα πράξεις δοκοῦσιν ἄσχολοι εἶναι, αἱ μὲν πολεμικαὶ καὶ παντελῶς (οὐδεὶς γὰρ αἱρεῖται τὸ πολεμεῖν τοῦ πολεμεῖν ἕνεκα, οὐδὲ παρασκευάζει πόλεμον· δόξαι γὰρ ἂν παντελῶς μιαιφόνος τις εἶναι, εἰ τοὺς φίλους πολεμίους ποιοῖτο, ἵνα μάχαι καὶ φόνοι γίγνοιντο)· ἔστι δὲ καὶ ἡ τοῦ πολι-

man needs other persons towards whom or with whose aid he may act justly, and so likewise do the temperate man and the brave man and the others, the wise man on the contrary can also contemplate by himself, and the more so the wiser he is; no doubt he will study better with the aid of fellow-workers, but still he is the most self-sufficient of men. Also the activity of contemplation may be held to be the only activity that is loved for its own sake: it produces no result beyond the actual act of contemplation, whereas from practical pursuits we look to secure some advantage, greater or smaller, beyond the action itself. Also happiness is thought to involve leisure; for we do business in order that we may have leisure, and carry on war in order that we may have peace. Now the practical virtues are exercised in politics or in warfare; but the pursuits of politics and war seem to be unleisured—those of war indeed entirely so, for no one desires to be at war for the sake of being at war, nor deliberately takes steps to cause a war: a man would be thought an utterly bloodthirsty character if he declared war on a friendly state for the sake of causing battles and

τικοῦ ἄσχολος, καὶ παρ' αὐτὸ τὸ πολιτεύεσθαι περιποιουμένη δυναστείας καὶ τιμὰς ἢ τήν γε εὐδαιμονίαν αὑτῷ καὶ τοῖς πολίταις, †ἑτέραν οὖσαν τῆς πολιτικῆς, ἣν καὶ ζητοῦμεν δῆλον ὡς ἑτέραν οὖσαν.† εἰ δὴ τῶν μὲν κατὰ τὰς ἀρετὰς πράξεων αἱ πολιτικαὶ καὶ πολεμικαὶ κάλλει καὶ μεγέθει προέχουσιν, αὗται δ' ἄσχολοι καὶ τέλους τινὸς ἐφίενται καὶ οὐ δι' αὑτὰς αἱρεταί εἰσιν, ἡ δὲ τοῦ νοῦ ἐνέργεια σπουδῇ τε διαφέρειν δοκεῖ θεωρητικὴ οὖσα, καὶ παρ' αὑτὴν οὐδενὸς ἐφίεσθαι τέλους, ἔχειν τε ἡδονὴν οἰκείαν (αὕτη δὲ συναύξει τὴν ἐνέργειαν), καὶ τὸ αὔταρκες δὴ καὶ σχολαστικὸν καὶ ἄτρυτον ὡς ἀνθρώπῳ, καὶ ὅσα ἄλλα τῷ μακαρίῳ ἀπονέμεται, τὰ κατὰ ταύτην τὴν ἐνέργειαν φαίνεται ὄντα· ἡ τελεία δὴ εὐδαιμονία αὕτη ἂν εἴη ἀνθρώπου, λαβοῦσα μῆκος βίου τέλειον· οὐδὲν γὰρ

massacres. But the activity of the politician also is unleisured, and aims at securing something beyond the mere participation in politics—positions of authority and honor, or, if the happiness of the politician himself and of his fellow-citizens, this happiness conceived as something distinct from political activity (indeed we are clearly investigating it as so distinct). If then among practical pursuits displaying the virtues, politics and war stand out preeminent in nobility and grandeur, and yet they are unleisured, and directed to some further end, not chosen for their own sakes: whereas the activity of the intellect is felt to excel in serious worth, consisting as it does in contemplation, and to aim at no end beyond itself, and also to contain a pleasure peculiar to itself, and therefore augmenting its activity: and if accordingly the attributes of this activity are found to be self-sufficiency, leisuredness, such freedom from fatigue as is possible for man, and all the other attributes of blessedness: it follows that it is the activity of the intellect that constitutes complete human happiness—provided it be granted a

ἀτελές ἐστι τῶν τῆς εὐδαιμονίας. ὁ δὲ τοιοῦτος ἂν εἴη βίος κρείττων ἢ κατ' ἄνθρωπον· οὐ γὰρ ᾗ ἄνθρωπός ἐστιν οὕτω βιώσεται, ἀλλ' ᾗ θεῖόν τι ἐν αὐτῷ ὑπάρχει· ὅσον δὲ διαφέρει τοῦτο τοῦ συνθέτου, τοσοῦτον καὶ ἡ ἐνέργεια τῆς κατὰ τὴν ἄλλην ἀρετήν. εἰ δὴ θεῖον ὁ νοῦς πρὸς τὸν ἄνθρωπον, καὶ ὁ κατὰ τοῦτον βίος θεῖος πρὸς τὸν ἀνθρώπινον βίον. οὐ χρὴ δὲ κατὰ τοὺς παραινοῦντας ἀνθρώπινα φρονεῖν ἄνθρωπον ὄντα οὐδὲ θνητὰ τὸν θνητόν, ἀλλ' ἐφ' ὅσον ἐνδέχεται ἀθανατίζειν καὶ πάντα ποιεῖν πρὸς τὸ ζῆν κατὰ τὸ κράτιστον τῶν ἐν αὐτῷ· εἰ γὰρ καὶ τῷ ὄγκῳ μικρόν ἐστι, δυνάμει καὶ τιμιότητι πολὺ μᾶλλον πάντων ὑπερέχει. δόξειε δ' ἂν καὶ εἶναι ἕκαστος τοῦτο, εἴπερ τὸ κύριον καὶ ἄμεινον· ἄτοπον οὖν γίνοιτ' ἄν, εἰ μὴ τὸν αὐτοῦ βίον αἱροῖτο ἀλλά τινος ἄλλου. τὸ

complete span of life, for nothing that belongs to happiness can be incomplete.

Such a life as this however will be higher than the human level: not in virtue of his humanity will a man achieve it, but in virtue of something within him that is divine; and by as much as this something is superior to his composite nature, by so much is its activity superior to the exercise of the other forms of virtue. If then the intellect is something divine in comparison with man, so is the life of the intellect divine in comparison with human life. Nor ought we to obey those who enjoin that a man should have man's thoughts and a mortal the thoughts of mortality, but we ought so far as possible to achieve immortality, and do all that man may to live in accordance with the highest thing in him; for though this be small in bulk, in power and value it far surpasses all the rest.

It may even be held that this is the true self of each, inasmuch as it is the dominant and better part; and therefore it would be a strange thing if a man should choose to live not his own life but the life of some other than himself.

λεχθέν τε πρότερον ἁρμόσει καὶ νῦν· τὸ γὰρ οἰκεῖον ἑκάστῳ τῇ φύσει κράτιστον καὶ ἥδιστόν ἐστιν ἑκάστῳ· καὶ τῷ ἀνθρώπῳ δὴ ὁ κατὰ τὸν νοῦν βίος, εἴπερ τοῦτο μάλιστα ἄνθρωπος· οὗτος ἄρα καὶ εὐδαιμονέστατος.

VIII Δευτέρως δ' ὁ κατὰ τὴν ἄλλην ἀρετήν· αἱ γὰρ κατὰ ταύτην ἐνέργειαι ἀνθρωπικαί· δίκαια γὰρ καὶ ἀνδρεῖα καὶ τὰ ἄλλα τὰ κατὰ τὰς ἀρετὰς πρὸς ἀλλήλους πράττομεν ἐν συναλλάγμασι καὶ χρείαις καὶ πράξεσι παντοίαις ἔν τε τοῖς πάθεσι διατηροῦντες τὸ πρέπον ἑκάστῳ, ταῦτα δ' εἶναι φαίνεται πάντα ἀνθρωπικά. ἔνια δὲ καὶ συμβαίνειν ἀπὸ τοῦ σώματος δοκεῖ, καὶ πολλὰ συνῳκειῶσθαι τοῖς πάθεσιν ἡ τοῦ ἤθους ἀρετή. συνέζευκται δὲ καὶ ἡ φρόνησις τῇ τοῦ ἤθους ἀρετῇ, καὶ αὕτη τῇ φρονήσει, εἴπερ αἱ μὲν τῆς φρονήσεως ἀρχαὶ κατὰ τὰς ἠθικάς εἰσιν ἀρετάς, τὸ

Moreover what was said before will apply here also: that which is best and most pleasant for each creature is that which is proper to the nature of each; accordingly the life of the intellect is the best and the pleasantest life for man, inasmuch as the intellect more than anything else is man; therefore this life will be the happiest.

The life of moral virtue, on the other hand, is happy only in a secondary degree. For the moral activities are purely human: Justice, I mean, Courage and the other virtues we display in our intercourse with our fellows, when we observe what is due to each in contracts and services and in our various actions, and in our emotions also; and all of these things seem to be purely human affairs. And some moral actions are thought to be the outcome of the physical constitution, and moral virtue is thought to have a close affinity in many respects with the passions. Moreover, Prudence is intimately connected with Moral Virtue, and this with Prudence, inasmuch as the first Principles which Prudence employs are determined by the Moral Virtues, and the right standard for the Moral Virtues

δ' ὀρθὸν τῶν ἠθικῶν κατὰ τὴν φρόνησιν. συνηρτημέναι δ' αὗται καὶ τοῖς πάθεσι περὶ τὸ σύνθετον ἂν εἶεν· αἱ δὲ τοῦ συνθέτου ἀρεταὶ ἀνθρωπικαί· καὶ ὁ βίος δὴ ὁ κατὰ αὐτὰς καὶ ἡ εὐδαιμονία. ἡ δὲ τοῦ νοῦ κεχωρισμένη· τοσοῦτον γὰρ περὶ αὐτῆς εἰρήσθω· διακριβῶσαι γὰρ μεῖζον τοῦ προκειμένου ἐστίν. δόξειε δ' ἂν καὶ τῆς ἐκτὸς χορηγίας ἐπὶ μικρὸν ἢ ἐπ' ἔλαττον δεῖσθαι τῆς ἠθικῆς· τῶν μὲν γὰρ ἀναγκαίων ἀμφοῖν χρεία καὶ ἐξ ἴσου ἔστω (εἰ καὶ μᾶλλον διαπονεῖ περὶ τὸ σῶμα ὁ πολιτικός, καὶ ὅσα τοιαῦτα)· μικρὸν γὰρ ἄν τι διαφέροι· πρὸς δὲ τὰς ἐνεργείας πολὺ διοίσει. τῷ μὲν γὰρ ἐλευθερίῳ δεήσει χρημάτων πρὸς τὸ πράττειν τὰ ἐλευθέρια, καὶ τῷ δικαίῳ δὴ εἰς τὰς ἀνταποδόσεις (αἱ γὰρ βουλήσεις ἄδηλοι, προσποιοῦνται δὲ καὶ οἱ μὴ δίκαιοι βούλεσθαι δικαιοπραγεῖν), τῷ ἀνδρείῳ δὲ δυνάμεως, εἴπερ

is determined by Prudence. But these being also connected with the passions are related to our composite nature; now the virtues of our composite nature are purely human; so therefore also is the life that manifests these virtues, and the happiness that belongs to it. Whereas the happiness that belongs to the intellect is separate: so much may be said about it here, for a full discussion of the matter is beyond the scope of our present purpose. And such happiness would appear to need but little external equipment, or less than the happiness based on moral virtue. Both, it may be granted, require the mere necessaries of life, and that in an equal degree (though the politician does as a matter of fact take more trouble about bodily requirements and so forth than the philosopher); for in this respect there may be little difference between them. But for the purpose of their special activities their requirements will differ widely. The liberal man will need wealth in order to do liberal actions, and so indeed will the just man in order to discharge his obligations (since mere intentions are invisible, and even the unjust pretend to wish

ἐπιτελεῖ τι τῶν κατὰ τὴν ἀρετήν, καὶ τῷ σώφρονι ἐξουσίας· πῶς γὰρ δῆλος ἔσται ἢ οὗτος ἢ τῶν ἄλλων τις; ἀμφισβητεῖταί τε πότερον κυριώτερον τῆς ἀρετῆς ἡ προαίρεσις ἢ αἱ πράξεις, ὡς ἐν ἀμφοῖν οὔσης. τὸ δὴ τέλειον δῆλον ὡς ἐν ἀμφοῖν ἂν εἴη· πρὸς δὲ τὰς πράξεις πολλῶν δεῖται, καὶ ὅσῳ ἂν μείζους ὦσι καὶ καλλίους, πλειόνων. τῷ δὲ θεωροῦντι οὐδενὸς τῶν τοιούτων πρός γε τὴν ἐνέργειαν χρεία, ἀλλ' ὡς εἰπεῖν καὶ ἐμπόδιά ἐστι πρός γε τὴν θεωρίαν· ᾗ δ' ἄνθρωπός ἐστι καὶ πλείοσι συζῇ, αἱρεῖται τὰ κατ' ἀρετὴν πράττειν· δεήσεται οὖν τῶν τοιούτων πρὸς τὸ ἀνθρωπεύεσθαι. —ἡ δὲ τελεία εὐδαιμονία ὅτι θεωρητική τίς ἐστιν ἐνέργεια, καὶ ἐντεῦθεν ἂν φανείη. τοὺς θεοὺς γὰρ μάλιστα ὑπειλήφαμεν μακαρίους καὶ εὐδαίμονας εἶναι· πράξεις δὲ ποίας ἀπονεῖμαι χρεὼν αὐτοῖς; πότερα τὰς δικαίας; ἢ γελοῖοι

to act justly); and the brave man will need strength if he is to perform any action displaying his virtue; and the temperate man opportunity for indulgence: otherwise how can he, or the possessor of any other virtue, show that he is virtuous? It is disputed also whether purpose or performance is the more important factor in virtue, as it is alleged to depend on both; now the perfection of virtue will clearly consist in both; but the performance of virtuous actions requires much outward equipment, and the more so the greater and more noble the actions are. But the student, so far as the pursuit of his activity is concerned, needs no external apparatus: on the contrary, worldly goods may almost be said to be a hindrance to contemplation; though it is true that, being a man and living in the society of others, he chooses to engage in virtuous action, and so will need external goods to carry on his life as a human being.

The following considerations also will show that perfect happiness is some form of contemplative activity. The gods, as we conceive them, enjoy supreme felicity and happiness. But what sort of

φανοῦνται συναλλάττοντες καὶ παρακαταθήκας ἀποδιδόντες καὶ ὅσα τοιαῦτα; ἀλλὰ τὰς ἀνδρείους, ὑπομένοντας τὰ φοβερὰ καὶ κινδυνεύοντας ὅτι καλόν; ἢ τὰς ἐλευθερίους; τίνι δὲ δώσουσιν; ἄτοπον δ' εἰ καὶ ἔσται αὐτοῖς νόμισμα ἤ τι τοιοῦτον. αἱ δὲ σώφρονες τί ἂν εἶεν; ἢ φορτικὸς ὁ ἔπαινος ὅτι οὐκ ἔχουσι φαύλας ἐπιθυμίας; διεξιοῦσι δὲ πάντα φαίνοιτ' ἂν τὰ περὶ τὰς πράξεις μικρὰ καὶ ἀνάξια θεῶν. ἀλλὰ μὴν ζῆν γε πάντες ὑπειλήφασιν αὐτούς, καὶ ἐνεργεῖν ἄρα· οὐ γὰρ δὴ καθεύδειν ὥσπερ τὸν Ἐνδυμίωνα. τῷ δὲ ζῶντι τοῦ πράττειν ἀφαιρουμένου, ἔτι δὲ μᾶλλον τοῦ ποιεῖν, τί λείπεται πλὴν θεωρία; ὥστε ἡ τοῦ θεοῦ ἐνέργεια, μακαριότητι διαφέρουσα, θεωρητικὴ ἂν εἴη. καὶ τῶν ἀνθρωπίνων δὴ ἡ ταύτῃ συγγενεστάτη εὐδαιμονικωτάτη. —σημεῖον δὲ καὶ τὸ μὴ μετέχειν τὰ λοιπὰ ζῷα εὐδαιμονίας,

actions can we attribute to them? Just actions? but will it not seem ridiculous to think of them as making contracts, restoring deposits and the like? Then brave actions—enduring terrors and running risks for the nobility of so doing? Or liberal actions? but to whom will they give? Besides, it would be absurd to suppose that they actually have a coinage or currency of some sort! And temperate actions—what will these mean in their case? surely it would be derogatory to praise them for not having evil desires! If we go through the list we shall find that all forms of virtuous conduct seem trifling and unworthy of the gods. Yet nevertheless they have always been conceived as, at all events, living, and therefore living actively, for we cannot suppose they are always asleep like Endymion. But for a living being, if we eliminate action, and a fortiori creative action, what remains save contemplation? It follows that the activity of God, which is transcendent in blessedness, is the activity of contemplation; and therefore among human activities that which is most akin to the divine activity of contemplation will be the greatest source of happiness.

τῆς τοιαύτης ἐνεργείας ἐστερημένα τελείως. τοῖς μὲν γὰρ θεοῖς ἅπας ὁ βίος μακάριος, τοῖς δ' ἀνθρώποις, ἐφ' ὅσον ὁμοίωμά τι τῆς τοιαύτης ἐνεργείας ὑπάρχει· τῶν δ' ἄλλων ζῴων οὐδὲν εὐδαιμονεῖ, ἐπειδὴ οὐδαμῇ κοινωνεῖ θεωρίας. ἐφ' ὅσον δὴ διατείνει ἡ θεωρία, καὶ ἡ εὐδαιμονία, καὶ οἷς μᾶλλον ὑπάρχει τὸ θεωρεῖν, καὶ εὐδαιμονεῖν, οὐ κατὰ συμβεβηκὸς ἀλλὰ κατὰ τὴν θεωρίαν· αὕτη γὰρ καθ' αὑτὴν τιμία. ὥστ' εἴη ἂν ἡ εὐδαιμονία θεωρία τις.

Δεήσει δὲ καὶ τῆς ἐκτὸς εὐημερίας ἀνθρώπῳ ὄντι· οὐ γὰρ αὐτάρκης ἡ φύσις πρὸς τὸ θεωρεῖν, ἀλλὰ δεῖ καὶ τὸ σῶμα ὑγιαίνειν καὶ τροφὴν καὶ τὴν λοιπὴν θεραπείαν ὑπάρχειν. οὐ μὴν οἰητέον γε πολλῶν καὶ μεγάλων δεήσεσθαι τὸν εὐδαιμονήσοντα, εἰ μὴ ἐνδέχεται ἄνευ τῶν ἐκτὸς ἀγαθῶν μακάριον εἶναι· οὐ γὰρ ἐν τῇ ὑπερβολῇ τὸ αὔταρκες οὐδ' ἡ πρᾶξις,

A further confirmation is that the lower animals cannot partake of happiness, because they are completely devoid of the contemplative activity. The whole of the life of the gods is blessed, and that of man is so in so far as it contains some likeness to the divine activity; but none of the other animals possess happiness, because they are entirely incapable of contemplation. Happiness therefore is co-extensive in its range with contemplation: the more a class of beings possesses the faculty of contemplation, the more it enjoys happiness, not as an accidental concomitant of contemplation but as inherent in it, since contemplation is valuable in itself. It follows that happiness is some form of contemplation.

But the philosopher being a man will also need external well—being, since man's nature is not self—sufficient for the activity of contemplation, but he must also have bodily health and a supply of food and other requirements. Yet if supreme blessedness is not possible without external goods, it must not be supposed that happiness will demand many or great possessions; for self-sufficiency does

δυνατὸν δὲ καὶ μὴ ἄρχοντα γῆς καὶ θαλάττης πράττειν τὰ καλά· καὶ γὰρ ἀπὸ μετρίων δύναιτ' ἄν τις πράττειν τὰ κατὰ τὴν ἀρετήν (τοῦτο δ' ἔστιν ἰδεῖν ἐναργῶς· οἱ γὰρ ἰδιῶται τῶν δυναστῶν οὐχ ἧττον δοκοῦσι τὰ ἐπιεικῆ πράττειν, ἀλλὰ καὶ μᾶλλον)· ἱκανὸν δὴ τοσαῦθ' ὑπάρχειν· ἔσται γὰρ ὁ βίος εὐδαίμων τοῦ κατὰ τὴν ἀρετὴν ἐνεργοῦντος. καὶ Σόλων δὲ τοὺς εὐδαίμονας ἴσως ἀπεφαίνετο καλῶς, εἰπὼν μετρίως τοῖς ἐκτὸς κεχορηγημένους, πεπραγότας δὲ τὰ κάλλισθ', ὡς ᾤετο, καὶ βεβιωκότας σωφρόνως· ἐνδέχεται γὰρ μέτρια κεκτημένους πράττειν ἃ δεῖ. ἔοικε δὲ καὶ Ἀναξαγόρας οὐ πλούσιον οὐδὲ δυνάστην ὑπολαβεῖν τὸν εὐδαίμονα, εἰπὼν ὅτι οὐκ ἂν θαυμάσειεν εἴ τις ἄτοπος φανείη τοῖς πολλοῖς· οὗτοι γὰρ κρίνουσι τοῖς ἐκτός, τούτων αἰσθανόμενοι μόνον. συμφωνεῖν δὴ τοῖς λόγοις ἐοίκασιν αἱ τῶν

not depend on excessive abundance, nor does moral conduct, and it is possible to perform noble deeds even without being ruler of land and sea: one can do virtuous acts with quite moderate resources. This may be clearly observed in experience: private citizens do not seem to be less but more given to doing virtuous actions than princes and potentates. It is sufficient then if moderate resources are forthcoming; for a life of virtuous activity will be essentially a happy life.

Solon also doubtless gave a good description of happiness, when he said that in his opinion those men were happy who, being moderately equipped with external goods, had performed noble exploits and had lived temperately; for it is possible for a man of but moderate possessions to do what is right. Anaxagoras again does not seem to have conceived the happy man as rich or powerful, since he says that he would not be surprised if he were to appear a strange sort of person in the eyes of the many; for most men judge by externals, which are all that they can perceive. So our theories seem to be in agreement with the opinions of the wise.

σοφῶν δόξαι. πίστιν μὲν οὖν καὶ τὰ τοιαῦτα ἔχει τινά, τὸ δ' ἀληθὲς ἐν τοῖς πρακτοῖς ἐκ τῶν ἔργων καὶ τοῦ βίου κρίνεται· ἐν τούτοις γὰρ τὸ κύριον. σκοπεῖν δὴ τὰ προειρημένα χρὴ ἐπὶ τὰ ἔργα καὶ τὸν βίον φέροντας, καὶ συναδόντων μὲν τοῖς ἔργοις ἀποδεκτέον, διαφωνούντων δὲ λόγους ὑποληπτέον. —ὁ δὲ κατὰ νοῦν ἐνεργῶν καὶ τοῦτον θεραπεύων καὶ διακείμενος ἄριστα καὶ θεοφιλέστατος ἔοικεν εἶναι. εἰ γάρ τις ἐπιμέλεια τῶν ἀνθρωπίνων ὑπὸ θεῶν γίνεται, ὥσπερ δοκεῖ, καὶ εἴη ἂν εὔλογον χαίρειν τε αὐτοὺς τῷ ἀρίστῳ καὶ τῷ συγγενεστάτῳ (τοῦτο δ' ἂν εἴη ὁ νοῦς) καὶ τοὺς ἀγαπῶντας μάλιστα τοῦτο καὶ τιμῶντας ἀντευποιεῖν ὡς τῶν φίλων αὐτοῖς ἐπιμελουμένους καὶ ὀρθῶς τε καὶ καλῶς πράττοντας. ὅτι δὲ πάντα ταῦτα τῷ σοφῷ μάλισθ' ὑπάρχει, οὐκ ἄδηλον. θεοφιλέ-

Such arguments then carry some degree of conviction; but it is by the practical experience of life and conduct that the truth is really tested, since it is ther that the final decision lies. We must therefore examine the conclusions we have advanced by bringing them to the test of the facts of life. If they are in harmony with the facts, we may accept them; if found to disagree, we must deem them mere theories.

And it seems likely that the man who pursues intellectual activity, and who cultivates his intellect and keeps that in the best condition, is also the man most beloved of the gods. For if, as is generally believed, the gods exercise some superintendence over human affairs, then it will be reasonable to suppose that they take pleasure in that part of man which is best and most akin to themselves, namely the intellect, and that they recompense with their favors those men who esteem and honor this most, because these care for the things dear to themselves, and act rightly and nobly. Now it is clear that all these attributes belong most of all to the wise man. He therefore is

στατος ἄρα. τὸν αὐτὸν δ' εἰκὸς καὶ εὐδαιμονέστατον· ὥστε κἂν οὕτως εἴη ὁ σοφὸς μάλιστ' εὐδαίμων.

IX Ἆρ' οὖν εἰ περὶ τούτων καὶ τῶν ἀρετῶν, ἔτι δὲ καὶ φιλίας καὶ ἡδονῆς ἱκανῶς εἴρηται τοῖς τύποις, τέλος ἔχειν οἰητέον τὴν προαίρεσιν, ἢ καθάπερ λέγεται, οὐκ ἔστιν ἐν τοῖς πρακτοῖς τέλος τὸ θεωρῆσαι ἕκαστα καὶ γνῶναι, ἀλλὰ μᾶλλον τὸ πράττειν αὐτά; οὐδὲ δὴ περὶ ἀρετῆς ἱκανὸν τὸ εἰδέναι, ἀλλ' ἔχειν καὶ χρῆσθαι πειρατέον, ἢ εἴ πως ἄλλως ἀγαθοὶ γινόμεθα. εἰ μὲν οὖν ἦσαν οἱ λόγοι αὐτάρκεις πρὸς τὸ ποιῆσαι ἐπιεικεῖς, "πολλοὺς ἂν μισθοὺς καὶ μεγάλους" δικαίως "ἔφερον" κατὰ τὸν Θέογνιν, καὶ ἔδει ἂν τούτους πορίσασθαι· νῦν δὲ φαίνονται προτρέψασθαι μὲν καὶ παρορμῆσαι τῶν νέων τοὺς ἐλευθερίους ἰσχύειν, ἦθός τ' εὐγενὲς καὶ ὡς ἀληθῶς φιλόκαλον ποιῆσαι ἂν κατοκώχιμον ἐκ

most beloved by the gods; and if so, he is naturally most happy. Here is another proof that the wise man is the happiest.

If then we have sufficiently discussed in their outlines the subjects of Happiness and of Virtue in its various forms, and also Friendship and Pleasure, may we assume that the investigation we proposed is now complete? Perhaps however, as we maintain, in the practical sciences the end is not to attain a theoretic knowledge of the various subjects, but rather to carry out our theories in action. If so, to know what virtue is is not enough; we must endeavor to possess and to practice it, or in some other manner actually ourselves to become good.

Now if discourses on ethics were sufficient in themselves to make men virtuous, 'large fees and many' (as Theognis says) 'would they win,' quite rightly, and to provide such discourses would be all that is wanted. But as it is, we see that although theories have power to stimulate and encourage generous youths, and, given an inborn nobility of character and a genuine love of what is noble, can make them susceptible to the influence of virtue,

τῆς ἀρετῆς, τοὺς δὲ πολλοὺς ἀδυνατεῖν πρὸς καλοκαγαθίαν προτρέψασθαι· οὐ γὰρ πεφύκασιν αἰδοῖ πειθαρχεῖν ἀλλὰ φόβῳ, οὐδ' ἀπέχεσθαι τῶν φαύλων διὰ τὸ αἰσχρὸν ἀλλὰ διὰ τὰς τιμωρίας· πάθει γὰρ ζῶντες τὰς οἰκείας ἡδονὰς διώκουσι καὶ δι' ὧν αὗται ἔσονται, φεύγουσι δὲ τὰς ἀντικειμένας λύπας, τοῦ δὲ καλοῦ καὶ ὡς ἀληθῶς ἡδέος οὐδ' ἔννοιαν ἔχουσιν, ἄγευστοι ὄντες. τοὺς δὴ τοιούτους τίς ἂν λόγος μεταρρυθμίσαι; οὐ γὰρ οἷόν τε ἢ οὐ ῥᾴδιον τὰ ἐκ παλαιοῦ τοῖς ἤθεσι κατειλημμένα λόγῳ μεταστῆσαι. ἀγαπητὸν δ' ἴσως ἐστὶν εἰ πάντων ὑπαρχόντων δι' ὧν ἐπιεικεῖς δοκοῦμεν γίνεσθαι, μεταλάβοιμεν τῆς ἀρετῆς. —γίνεσθαι δ' ἀγαθοὺς οἴονται οἱ μὲν φύσει, οἱ δ' ἔθει, οἱ δὲ διδαχῇ. τὸ μὲν οὖν τῆς φύσεως δῆλον ὡς οὐκ ἐφ' ἡμῖν [ὑπάρχει], ἀλλὰ διά τινας θείας αἰτίας τοῖς ὡς ἀληθῶς εὐτυχέσιν ὑπάρχει·

yet they are powerless to stimulate the mass of mankind to moral nobility. For it is the nature of the many to be amenable to fear but not to a sense of honor, and to abstain from evil not because of its baseness but because of the penalties it entails; since, living as they do by passion, they pursue the pleasures akin to their nature, and the things that will procure those pleasures, and avoid the opposite pains, but have not even a notion of what is noble and truly pleasant, having never tasted true pleasure. What theory then can reform the natures of men like these? To dislodge by argument habits long firmly rooted in their characters is difficult if not impossible. We may doubtless think ourselves fortunate if we attain some measure of virtue when all the things believed to make men virtuous are ours.

Now some thinkers hold that virtue is a gift of nature; others think we become good by habit, others that we can be taught to be good. Natural endowment is obviously not under our control; it is bestowed on those who are fortunate, in the true sense, by some divine dispensation. Again, theory and teaching are not, I fear, equally efficacious in all

ὁ δὲ λόγος καὶ ἡ διδαχὴ μή ποτ' οὐκ ἐν ἅπασιν ἰσχύει, ἀλλὰ δεῖ προδιειργάσθαι τοῖς ἔθεσι τὴν τοῦ ἀκροατοῦ ψυχὴν πρὸς τὸ καλῶς χαίρειν καὶ μισεῖν, ὥσπερ γῆν τὴν θρέψουσαν τὸ σπέρμα. οὐ γὰρ ἂν ἀκούσειε λόγου ἀποτρέποντος οὐδ' ἂν συνείη ὁ κατὰ πάθος ζῶν· τὸν δ' οὕτως ἔχοντα πῶς οἷόν τε μεταπεῖσαι; ὅλως τ' οὐ δοκεῖ λόγῳ ὑπείκειν τὸ πάθος ἀλλὰ βίᾳ. δεῖ δὴ τὸ ἦθος προϋπάρχειν πως οἰκεῖον τῆς ἀρετῆς, στέργον τὸ καλὸν καὶ δυσχεραῖνον τὸ αἰσχρόν. ἐκ νέου δ' ἀγωγῆς ὀρθῆς τυχεῖν πρὸς ἀρετὴν χαλεπὸν μὴ ὑπὸ τοιούτοις τραφέντα νόμοις· τὸ γὰρ σωφρόνως καὶ καρτερικῶς ζῆν οὐχ ἡδὺ τοῖς πολλοῖς, ἄλλως τε καὶ νέοις· διὸ νόμοις δεῖ τετάχθαι τὴν τροφὴν καὶ τὰ ἐπιτηδεύματα· οὐκ ἔσται γὰρ λυπηρὰ συνήθη γενόμενα. οὐχ ἱκανὸν δ' ἴσως νέους ὄντας τροφῆς καὶ ἐπιμελείας τυχεῖν

cases: the soil must have been previously tilled if it is to foster the seed, the mind of the pupil must have been prepared by the cultivation of habits, so as to like and dislike aright. For he that lives at the dictates of passion will not hear nor understand the reasoning of one who tries to dissuade him; but if so, how can you change his mind by argument?

And, speaking generally, passion seems not to be amenable to reason, but only to force.

We must therefore by some means secure that the character shall have at the outset a natural affinity for virtue, loving what is noble and hating what is base. And it is difficult to obtain a right education in virtue from youth up without being brought up under right laws; for to live temperately and hardily is not pleasant to most men, especially when young; hence the nurture and exercises of the young should be regulated by law, since temperance and hardiness will not be painful when they have become habitual. But doubtless it is not enough for people to receive the right nurture and discipline in youth; they must also practice the lessons they have learnt, and confirm them by habit, when they are grown

ὀρθῆς, ἀλλ' ἐπειδὴ καὶ ἀνδρωθέντας δεῖ ἐπιτηδεύειν αὐτὰ καὶ ἐθίζεσθαι, καὶ περὶ ταῦτα δεοίμεθ' ἄν νόμων, καὶ ὅλως δὴ περὶ πάντα τὸν βίον· οἱ γὰρ πολλοὶ ἀνάγκῃ μᾶλλον ἢ λόγῳ πειθαρχοῦσι καὶ ζημίαις ἢ τῷ καλῷ. διόπερ οἴονταί τινες τοὺς νομοθετοῦντας δεῖν μὲν παρακαλεῖν ἐπὶ τὴν ἀρετὴν καὶ προτρέπεσθαι τοῦ καλοῦ χάριν, ὡς ὑπακουσομένων τῶν ἐπιεικῶς τοῖς ἔθεσι προηγμένων, ἀπειθοῦσι δὲ καὶ ἀφυεστέροις οὖσι κολάσεις τε καὶ τιμωρίας ἐπιτιθέναι, τοὺς δ' ἀνιάτους ὅλως ἐξορίζειν· τὸν μὲν γὰρ ἐπιεικῆ πρὸς τὸ καλὸν ζῶντα τῷ λόγῳ πειθαρχήσειν, τὸν δὲ φαῦλον ἡδονῆς ὀρεγόμενον λύπῃ κολάζεσθαι ὥσπερ ὑποζύγιον. διὸ καί φασι δεῖν τοιαύτας γίνεσθαι τὰς λύπας αἳ μάλιστ' ἐναντιοῦνται ταῖς ἀγαπωμέναις ἡδοναῖς. —εἰ δ' οὖν, καθάπερ εἴρηται, τὸν ἐσόμενον ἀγαθὸν τραφῆναι καλῶς δεῖ καὶ

up. Accordingly we shall need laws to regulate the discipline of adults as well, and in fact the whole life of the people generally; for the many are more amenable to compulsion and punishment than to reason and to moral ideals. Hence some persons hold, that while it is proper for the lawgiver to encourage and exhort men to virtue on moral grounds, in the expectation that those who have had a virtuous moral upbringing will respond, yet he is bound to impose chastisement and penalties on the disobedient and ill-conditioned, and to banish the incorrigible out of the state altogether. For (they argue) although the virtuous man, who guides his life by moral ideals, will be obedient to reason, the base, whose desires are fixed on pleasure, must be chastised by pain, like a beast of burden. This indeed is the ground for the view that the pains and penalties for transgressors should be such as are most opposed to their favorite pleasures.

But to resume: if, as has been said, in order to be good a man must have been properly educated and trained, and must subsequently continue to follow virtuous habits of life, and to do nothing base

ἐθισθῆναι, εἶθ' οὕτως ἐν ἐπιτηδεύμασιν ἐπιεικέσι ζῆν καὶ μήτ' ἄκοντα μήθ' ἑκόντα πράττειν τὰ φαῦλα, ταῦτα δὲ γίγνοιτ' ἂν βιουμένοις κατά τινα νοῦν καὶ τάξιν ὀρθήν, ἔχουσαν ἰσχύν. ἡ μὲν οὖν πατρικὴ πρόσταξις οὐκ ἔχει τὸ ἰσχυρὸν οὐδὲ τὸ ἀναγκαῖον, οὐδὲ δὴ ὅλως ἡ ἑνὸς ἀνδρός, μὴ βασιλέως ὄντος ἤ τινος τοιούτου· ὁ δὲ νόμος ἀναγκαστικὴν ἔχει δύναμιν, λόγος ὢν ἀπό τινος φρονήσεως καὶ νοῦ. καὶ τῶν μὲν ἀνθρώπων ἐχθαίρουσι τοὺς ἐναντιουμένους ταῖς ὁρμαῖς, κἂν ὀρθῶς αὐτὸ δρῶσιν· ὁ δὲ νόμος οὐκ ἔστιν ἐπαχθὴς τάττων τὸ ἐπιεικές. ἐν μόνῃ δὲ τῇ Λακεδαιμονίων πόλει <ἢ> μετ' ὀλίγων ὁ νομοθέτης ἐπιμέλειαν δοκεῖ πεποιῆσθαι τροφῆς τε καὶ ἐπιτηδευμάτων· ἐν δὲ ταῖς πλείσταις τῶν πόλεων ἐξημέληται περὶ τῶν τοιούτων, καὶ ζῇ ἕκαστος ὡς βούλεται, κυκλωπικῶς θεμιστεύων "παίδων ἠδ'

whether voluntarily or involuntarily, then this will be secured if men's lives are regulated by a certain intelligence, and by a right system, invested with adequate sanctions. Now paternal authority has not the power to compel obedience, nor indeed, speaking generally, has the authority of any individual unless he be a king or the like; but law on the other hand is a rule, emanating from a certain wisdom and intelligence, that has compulsory force. Men are hated when they thwart people's inclinations, even though they do so rightly, whereas law can enjoin virtuous conduct without being invidious. But Sparta appears to be the only or almost the only state in which the lawgiver has paid attention to the nurture and exercises of the citizens; in most states such matters have been entirely neglected, and every man lives as he likes, in Cyclops fashion 'laying down the law for children and for spouse.'

The best thing is then that there should be a proper system of public regulation; but when the matter is neglected by the community, it would seem to be the duty of the individual to assist his

ἀλόχου". κράτιστον μὲν οὖν τὸ γίγνεσθαι κοινὴν ἐπιμέλειαν καὶ ὀρθήν· κοινῇ δ' ἐξαμελουμένων ἑκάστῳ δόξειεν ἂν προσήκειν τοῖς σφετέροις τέκνοις καὶ φίλοις εἰς ἀρετὴν συμβάλλεσθαι, καὶ δρᾶν αὐτὸ δύνασθαι, ἢ προαιρεῖσθαί γε. μᾶλλον δ' ἂν τοῦτο δύνασθαι δόξειεν ἐκ τῶν εἰρημένων νομοθετικὸς γενόμενος· αἱ μὲν γὰρ κοιναὶ ἐπιμέλειαι δῆλον ὅτι διὰ νόμων γίγνονται, ἐπιεικεῖς δ' αἱ διὰ τῶν σπουδαίων· γεγραμμένων δ' ἢ ἀγράφων, οὐδὲν ἂν δόξειε διαφέρειν, οὐδὲ δι' ὧν εἷς ἢ πολλοὶ παιδευθήσονται, ὥσπερ οὐδ' ἐπὶ μουσικῆς καὶ γυμναστικῆς καὶ τῶν ἄλλων ἐπιτηδευμάτων. ὥσπερ γὰρ ἐν ταῖς πόλεσιν ἐνισχύει τὰ νόμιμα καὶ τὰ ἔθη, οὕτω καὶ ἐν οἰκίαις οἱ πατρικοὶ λόγοι καὶ τὰ ἔθη, καὶ ἔτι μᾶλλον διὰ τὴν συγγένειαν καὶ τὰς εὐεργεσίας· προϋπάρχουσι γὰρ στέργοντες καὶ εὐπειθεῖς τῇ φύσει. ἔτι δὲ

own children and friends to attain virtue, or even if not able to do so successfully, at all events to make this his aim. But it would seem to follow from what has been said before, that he will be more likely to be successful in this if he has acquired the science of legislation. Public regulations in any case must clearly be established by law, and only good laws will produce good regulations; but it would not seem to make any difference whether these laws are written or unwritten, or whether they are to regulate the education of a single person or of a number of people, any more than in the case of music or athletics or any other form of training. Paternal exhortations and family habits have authority in the household, just as legal enactments and national customs have authority in the state, and the more so on account of the ties of relationship and of benefits conferred that unite the head of the household to its other members: he can count on their natural affection and obedience at the outset. Moreover individual treatment is better than a common system, in education as in medicine. As a general rule rest and fasting are good for a fever,

καὶ διαφέρουσιν αἱ καθ' ἕκαστον παιδεῖαι τῶν κοινῶν, ὥσπερ ἐπὶ ἰατρικῆς· καθόλου μὲν γὰρ τῷ πυρέττοντι συμφέρει ἡσυχία καὶ ἀσιτία, τινὶ δ' ἴσως οὔ, ὅ τε πυκτικὸς ἴσως οὐ πᾶσι τὴν αὐτὴν μάχην περιτίθησιν. ἐξακριβοῦσθαι δὴ δόξειεν ἂν μᾶλλον τὸ καθ' ἕκαστον ἰδίας τῆς ἐπιμελείας γινομένης· μᾶλλον γὰρ τοῦ προσφόρου τυγχάνει ἕκαστος. ἀλλ' ἐπιμεληθείη ἂν ἄριστα καθ' ἕνα καὶ ἰατρὸς καὶ γυμναστὴς καὶ πᾶς ἄλλος ὁ καθόλου εἰδώς τί πᾶσιν ἢ τοῖς τοιοῖσδε· τοῦ κοινοῦ γὰρ αἱ ἐπιστῆμαι λέγονταί τε καὶ εἰσίν. οὐ μὴν ἀλλ' ἑνός τινος οὐδὲν ἴσως κωλύει καλῶς ἐπιμεληθῆναι καὶ ἀνεπιστήμονα ὄντα, τεθεαμένον δ' ἀκριβῶς τὰ συμβαίνοντα ἐφ' ἑκάστῳ δι' ἐμπειρίαν, καθάπερ καὶ ἰατροὶ ἔνιοι δοκοῦσιν ἑαυτῶν ἄριστοι εἶναι, ἑτέρῳ οὐδὲν ἂν δυνάμενοι ἐπαρκέσαι. οὐδὲν δ' ἧττον ἴσως τῷ γε βουλομένῳ

but they may not be best for a particular case; and presumably a professor of boxing does not impose the same style of fighting on all his pupils. It would appear then that private attention gives more accurate results in particular cases, for the particular subject is more likely to get the treatment that suits him. But a physician or trainer or any other director can best treat a particular person if he has a general knowledge of what is good for everybody, or for other people of the same kind: for the sciences deal with what is universal, as their names imply. Not but what it is possible no doubt for a particular individual to be successfully treated by someone who is not a scientific expert, but has an empirical knowledge based on careful observation of the effects of various forms of treatment upon the person in question; just as some people appear to be their own best doctors, though they could not do any good to someone else. But nevertheless it would doubtless be agreed that anyone who wishes to make himself a professional and a man of science must advance to general principles, and acquaint himself with these by the proper method:

τεχνικῷ γενέσθαι καὶ θεωρητικῷ ἐπὶ τὸ καθόλου βαδιστέον εἶναι δόξειεν ἄν, κἀκεῖνο γνωριστέον ὡς ἐνδέχεται· εἴρηται γὰρ ὅτι περὶ τοῦθ' αἱ ἐπιστῆμαι. τάχα δὴ καὶ τῷ βουλομένῳ δι' ἐπιμελείας βελτίους ποιεῖν, εἴτε πολλοὺς εἴτ' ὀλίγους, νομοθετικῷ πειρατέον γενέσθαι, εἰ διὰ νόμων ἀγαθοὶ γενοίμεθ' ἄν. ὅντινα γὰρ οὖν καὶ τὸν προτεθέντα διαθεῖναι καλῶς οὐκ ἔστι τοῦ τυχόντος, ἀλλ' εἴπερ τινος, τοῦ εἰδότος, ὥσπερ ἐπ' ἰατρικῆς καὶ τῶν λοιπῶν ὧν ἐστιν ἐπιμέλειά τις καὶ φρόνησις. ἆρ' οὖν μετὰ τοῦτο ἐπισκεπτέον πόθεν ἢ πῶς νομοθετικὸς γένοιτ' ἄν τις; ἢ καθάπερ ἐπὶ τῶν ἄλλων, παρὰ τῶν πολιτικῶν; μόριον γὰρ ἐδόκει τῆς πολιτικῆς εἶναι. ἢ οὐχ ὅμοιον φαίνεται ἐπὶ τῆς πολιτικῆς καὶ τῶν λοιπῶν ἐπιστημῶν τε καὶ δυνάμεων; ἐν μὲν γὰρ ταῖς ἄλλαις οἱ αὐτοὶ φαίνονται τάς τε δυνάμεις παραδι-

for science, as we said, deals with the universal. So presumably a man who wishes to make other people better (whether few or many) by discipline, must endeavor to acquire the science of legislation—assuming that it is possible to make us good by laws. For to mold aright the character of any and every person that presents himself is not a task that can be done by anybody, but only (if at all) by the man with scientific knowledge, just as is the case in medicine and the other professions involving a system of treatment and the exercise of prudence.

Is not then the next question to consider from whom or how the science of legislation can be learnt? Perhaps, like other subjects, from the experts, namely the politicians; for we saw that legislation who is a branch of political science. But possibly it may seem that political science is unlike the other sciences and faculties. In these the persons who impart a knowledge of the faculty are the same as those who practice it, for instance physicians and painters; but in politics the sophists, who profess to teach the science, never practice it. It is practiced by the politicians, who would appear to

δόντες καὶ ἐνεργοῦντες ἀπ' αὐτῶν, οἷον ἰατροὶ καὶ γραφεῖς· τὰ δὲ πολιτικὰ ἐπαγγέλλονται μὲν διδάσκειν οἱ σοφισταί, πράττει δ' αὐτῶν οὐδείς, ἀλλ' οἱ πολιτευόμενοι, οἳ δόξαιεν ἂν δυνάμει τινὶ τοῦτο πράττειν καὶ ἐμπειρίᾳ μᾶλλον ἢ διανοίᾳ· οὔτε γὰρ γράφοντες οὔτε λέγοντες περὶ τῶν τοιούτων φαίνονται (καίτοι κάλλιον ἦν ἴσως ἢ λόγους δικανικούς τε καὶ δημηγορικούς), οὐδ' αὖ πολιτικοὺς πεποιηκότες τοὺς σφετέρους υἱεῖς ἤ τινας ἄλλους τῶν φίλων. εὔλογον δ' ἦν, εἴπερ ἐδύναντο· οὔτε γὰρ ταῖς πόλεσιν ἄμεινον οὐδὲν κατέλιπον ἄν, οὔθ' αὑτοῖς ὑπάρξαι προέλοιντ' ἂν μᾶλλον τῆς τοιαύτης δυνάμεως, οὐδὲ δὴ τοῖς φιλτάτοις. οὐ μὴν μικρόν γε ἔοικεν ἡ ἐμπειρία συμβάλλεσθαι· οὐδὲ γὰρ ἐγίγνοντ' ἂν διὰ τῆς πολιτικῆς συνηθείας πολιτικοί· διὸ τοῖς ἐφιεμένοις περὶ πολιτικῆς εἰδέναι προσδεῖν ἔοικεν ἐμπει-

rely more upon a sort of empirical skill than on the exercise of abstract intelligence; for we do not see them writing or lecturing about political principles (though this might be a more honorable employment than composing forensic and parliamentary speeches), nor yet do we notice that they have made their own sons or any others of their friends into statesmen. Yet we should expect them to have done so had they been able, for they could have bequeathed no more valuable legacy to their countries, nor is there any quality they would choose for themselves, and therefore for those nearest to them, to possess, in preference to political capacity. Not that experience does not seem to contribute considerably to political success; otherwise men would never have become statesmen merely through practical association with politics; so it would appear that those who aspire to a scientific knowledge of politics require practical experience as well as study. On the other hand those sophists who profess to teach politics are found to be very far from doing so successfully. In fact they are absolutely ignorant of the very nature of the science and

ρίας. τῶν δὲ σοφιστῶν οἱ ἐπαγγελλόμενοι λίαν φαίνονται πόρρω εἶναι τοῦ διδάξαι· ὅλως γὰρ οὐδὲ ποῖόν τί ἐστιν ἢ περὶ ποῖα ἴσασιν· οὐ γὰρ ἂν τὴν αὐτὴν τῇ ῥητορικῇ οὐδὲ χείρω ἐτίθεσαν, οὐδ' ἂν ᾤοντο ῥᾴδιον εἶναι τὸ νομοθετῆσαι συναγαγόντι τοὺς εὐδοκιμοῦντας τῶν νόμων· ἐκλέξασθαι γὰρ εἶναι τοὺς ἀρίστους, ὥσπερ οὐδὲ τὴν ἐκλογὴν οὖσαν συνέσεως καὶ τὸ κρῖναι ὀρθῶς μέγιστον, ὥσπερ ἐν τοῖς κατὰ μουσικήν· οἱ γὰρ ἔμπειροι περὶ ἕκαστα κρίνουσιν ὀρθῶς τὰ ἔργα, καὶ δι' ὧν ἢ πῶς ἐπιτελεῖται συνιᾶσιν, καὶ ποῖα ποίοις συνᾴδει· τοῖς δ' ἀπείροις ἀγαπητὸν τὸ μὴ διαλανθάνειν εἰ εὖ ἢ κακῶς πεποίηται τὸ ἔργον, ὥσπερ ἐπὶ γραφικῆς. οἱ δὲ νόμοι τῆς πολιτικῆς ἔργοις ἐοίκασιν· πῶς οὖν ἐκ τούτων νομοθετικὸς γένοιτ' ἄν τις, ἢ τοὺς ἀρίστους κρίναι; οὐ γὰρ φαίνονται οὐδ' ἰατρικοὶ

of the subjects with which it deals; otherwise they would not class it as identical with, or even inferior to, the art of rhetoric. Nor would they imagine that it is easy to frame a constitution by making a collection of such existing laws as are reputed to be good ones, on the assumption that one can then select the best among them; as if even this selection did not call for understanding, and as if to judge correctly were not a very difficult task, just as much as it is for instance in music. It is only the experts in an art who can judge correctly the productions of that art, and who understand the means and the method by which perfection is attained, and know which elements harmonize with which; amateurs may be content if they can discern whether the general result produced is good or bad, for example in the art of painting. Laws are the product, so to speak, of the art of politics; how then can a mere collection of laws teach a man the science of legislation, or make him able to judge which of them are the best? We do not see men becoming expert physicians from a study of medical handbooks. Yet medical writers attempt to describe not only

ἐκ τῶν συγγραμμάτων γίνεσθαι. καίτοι πειρῶνταί γε λέγειν οὐ μόνον τὰ θεραπεύματα, ἀλλὰ καὶ ὡς ἰαθεῖεν ἂν καὶ ὡς δεῖ θεραπεύειν ἑκάστους, διελόμενοι τὰς ἕξεις· ταῦτα δὲ τοῖς μὲν ἐμπείροις ὠφέλιμα εἶναι δοκεῖ, τοῖς δ' ἀνεπιστήμοσιν ἀχρεῖα. ἴσως οὖν καὶ τῶν νόμων καὶ τῶν πολιτειῶν αἱ συναγωγαὶ τοῖς μὲν δυναμένοις θεωρῆσαι καὶ κρῖναι τί καλῶς ἢ τοὐναντίον καὶ ποῖα ποίοις ἁρμόττει εὔχρηστ' ἂν εἴη· τοῖς δ' ἄνευ ἕξεως τὰ τοιαῦτα διεξιοῦσι τὸ μὲν κρίνειν καλῶς οὐκ ἂν ὑπάρχοι, εἰ μὴ ἄρα αὐτόματον, εὐσυνετώτεροι δ' εἰς ταῦτα τάχ' ἂν γένοιντο. παραλιπόντων οὖν τῶν προτέρων ἀνερεύνητον τὸ περὶ τῆς νομοθεσίας, αὐτοὺς ἐπισκέψασθαι μᾶλλον βέλτιον ἴσως, καὶ ὅλως δὴ περὶ πολιτείας, ὅπως εἰς δύναμιν ἡ περὶ τὰ ἀνθρώπεια φιλοσοφία τελειωθῇ. πρῶτον μὲν οὖν εἴ τι κατὰ

general courses of treatment, but also methods of cure and modes of treatment for particular sorts of patients, classified according to their various habits of body; and their treatises appear to be of value for men who have had practical experience, though they are useless for the novice. Very possibly therefore collections of laws and constitutions may be serviceable to students capable of studying them critically, and judging what measures are valuable or the reverse, and what kind of institutions are suited to what national characteristics. But those who peruse such compilations without possessing a trained faculty cannot be capable of judging them correctly, unless they do so by instinct, though they may very likely sharpen their political intelligence.

As then the question of legislation has been left uninvestigated by previous thinkers, it will perhaps be well if we consider it for ourselves, together with the whole question of the constitution of the State, in order to complete as far as possible our philosophy of human affairs.

We will begin then by attempting a review of any pronouncements of value contributed by our

μέρος εἴρηται καλῶς ὑπὸ τῶν προγενεστέρων πειραθῶμεν ἐπελθεῖν, εἶτα ἐκ τῶν συνηγμένων πολιτειῶν θεωρῆσαι τὰ ποῖα σῴζει καὶ φθείρει τὰς πόλεις καὶ τὰ ποῖα ἑκάστας τῶν πολιτειῶν, καὶ διὰ τίνας αἰτίας αἱ μὲν καλῶς, αἱ δὲ τοὐναντίον πολιτεύονται· θεωρηθέντων γὰρ τούτων τάχ᾽ ἂν μᾶλλον συνίδοιμεν καὶ ποία πολιτεία ἀρίστη, καὶ πῶς ἑκάστη ταχθεῖσα, καὶ τίσι νόμοις καὶ ἔθεσι χρωμένη. λέγωμεν οὖν ἀρξάμενοι.

predecessors in this or that branch of the subject; and then on the basis of our collection of constitutions we will consider what institutions are preservative and what destructive of states in general, and of the different forms of constitution in particular, and what are the reasons which cause some states to be well governed and others the contrary. For after studying these questions we shall perhaps be in a better position to discern what is the best constitution absolutely, and what are the best regulations, laws, and customs for any given form of constitution. Let us then begin our discussion.

FURTHER READING

There is an immense amount of literature about Aristotle and the *Ethics*. We can only list a few publications here for those who would like to delve deeper into the subject.

The standard edition of the text is *Aristotelis Ethica Nicomachea*, ed. Ingram Bywater (Oxford 1894, reprinted many times). The complete corpus of Aristotelian texts was published in two volumes by Immanuel Bekker in 1831; all following editions adhere to Bekker's page numbering. Jonathan Barnes published a translation of the entire corpus, also in two volumes, on the basis of a translation that appeared between 1912 and 1954: *The Complete Works of Aristotle*, The Revised Oxford Translation, ed. Jonathan Barnes (Princeton 1984). In the Loeb

Classical Library the bilingual edition of H. Rackham first appeared as volume 73 in 1926; this is the translation used in this book.

In *Aristotle the Philosopher* (Oxford, 1981) John L. Ackrill provides a concise overview of Aristotle's work. *The Cambridge Companion to Aristotle*, ed. Jonathan Barnes (Cambridge 1995), provides chapters covering the whole oeuvre. Specifically for the *Ethics* there is the *Cambridge Companion to Aristotle's Nicomachean Ethics*, ed. Ronald Polansky (Cambridge 2014). A deservedly famous analysis of Aristotle's ethics is to be found in Martha C. Nussbaum, *The Fragility of Goodness: Luck and Ethics in Greek Tragedy and Philosophy* (Cambridge 1986). A particularly appealing book is Armand Marie Leroi, *The Lagoon: How Aristotle Invented Science* (London 2014).

P. G.

**ALSO FROM
AIORA PRESS:**

Myths Behind Words

GREEK MYTHOLOGY IN ENGLISH WORDS AND EXPRESSIONS

Compiled by Alexander Zaphiriou
Illustrated by Panagiotis Stavropoulos

This collection retells the myths behind common words and expressions in English, bringing to life the heroes, monsters and gods whose deeds and battles have left a hidden mark on our language.

AN ANTHOLOGY
Words of Wisdom from Ancient Greece

BILINGUAL EDITION

Translated by Alexander Zaphiriou
Illustrated by Panagiotis Stavropoulos

Words of Wisdom from Ancient Greece gathers the best of a thousand years of philosophy, history and literature, in a compilation of writing spanning from 800 BCE to 200 CE. This survey of ancient wisdom offers guidance for a life well lived from luminaries of Greece's legendary past.

EPICTETUS
Manual
on the Art of Living
BILINGUAL EDITION

Translated by P.E. Matheson

'*Of all existing things, some are in our power, and others are not in our power.*' So begins the *Manual* or *Enchiridion* of Epictetus. The *Manual*, considered to be the pinnacle of Stoic philosophy, addresses living with integrity, self-management and personal freedom.

EPICURUS
In Pursuit of Pleasure
BILINGUAL EDITION

Translated by Cyril Bailey

This volume contains Cyril Bailey's masterly, classic translations of the most important surviving writing of Epicurus and offers the contemporary reader a comprehensive overview of Epicurean Ethics, his philosophy on what matters in life and how we should live.

HIPPOCRATES
Aphorisms
BILINGUAL EDITION

Translated by W.H.S. Jones

Hippocrates of Kos is credited with being the first healer to separate the discipline of medicine from religion, arguing that disease was not a punishment inflicted by the gods but rather the product of environmental factors, diet and lifestyle.

PLATO
The Apology of Socrates BILINGUAL EDITION
Translated by Harold North Fowler

Socrates was seventy years old in the spring of 399 BCE, when he stood trial on charges of impiety and corrupting the youth of Athens. His defence speech, as reproduced in Plato's *Apology*, stands throughout the ages as a beacon of moral integrity, justice and democracy.

PYTHAGORAS
The Golden Verses BILINGUAL EDITION
Translated by David Connolly

The essence of Pythagoras' teachings is contained in *The Golden Verses*. Functioning as admonitions, they link the human with the divine element and determine the point at which both elements converge to reveal how we might ourselves attain this supreme virtue in our everyday lives.